JOHN STOTT'S RIGHT HAND
The untold story of Frances Whitehead
EXPANDED AND UPDATED

Julia E M Cameron

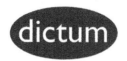

© Julia E M Cameron 2020
Dictum Press, Oxford, UK
www.dictumpress.com

First edition published in the UK by Piquant, Carlisle, 2014
This second edition published in the UK by Dictum, Oxford

Unless otherwise stated, all scripture references are taken from the New International Version. Copyright © 1973, 1978, 1984 by International Bible Society. Published by Hodder & Stoughton Ltd.

All scripture quotations marked KJV are taken from the King James Version. Crown copyright.

British Library Cataloguing Data, A catalogue record for this book is available from the British Library.

ISBN 978-1-9996621-7-2

Cover by Luz Design. *www.projectluz.com*

Cover image: Frances Whitehead with John Stott in his study-cum-sitting-room © Kieran Dodds 2007. *www.kierandodds.com*

Malvern Girls' College © Malvern St James archives

With John Stott at Buckingham Palace © Charles Green

Ten Commandments © Widecombe History Group

Whitehead Family Grave © Williams & Triggs, Newton Abbot

In gratitude for my parents,

Cam and Valerie

'John Stott was preaching the night I was converted and he has been my teacher ever since, not only by word but by example. He has obviously been the greatest influence in my life. Those who have influenced me most have always borne the hallmark of authenticity, that is of Christlikeness . . . So much of Christian truth is summed up in the amazing condescension of John 14:21.'

Frances Whitehead, January 2014

'Successive Study Assistants have basically fallen in love with Frances, and have realized that Uncle John could never have done what he did without her. It has been one of the greatest Christian partnerships of the twentieth century.'

Roy McCloughry, First Study Assistant 1977-78; National Disability Advisor in the Church of England; Tutor in Ethics, St. John's College, Nottingham

'Frances Whitehead was as remarkable in her way as John Stott was in his way. John was the gold standard and Frances matched it again and again. I loved Frances's personal spiritual life, her prayerfulness, her devotion to knowing and loving Christ, her hunger for biblical teaching, her desire for Christian community.'

Mark Labberton, Study Assistant 1980-81; President, Fuller Seminary, Southern California

'I have thought that Frances's loyalty to John is the best human example of *agape* that I have ever witnessed. And of course her example of 'omnicompetence' shall never be excelled. However her prior vocation has been to serve Christ and his church, and this she has done with self-sacrificial devotion, boundless energy and unequalled efficiency.'

Stephen Andrews, Study Assistant 1984-86; Bishop of Algoma, Province of Ontario, Canada

'Frances and Uncle John shared a wonderful partnership – platonic and professional, deep and affectionate. Their fifty-five-year relationship started formally, with Frances referring only to 'Mr Stott', but became much less formal, with their embracing on occasion with a warm hug and kiss on the cheek.'

Matthew Smith, Study Assistant 2002-05; a principal advisor at KPMG

CONTENTS

Published in association with

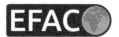

Evangelical Fellowship in
the Anglican Communion

Editorial note

Terms have been left in their original form. While it now sounds quaint to talk of a 'nursery class' for new Christians, it seemed better to leave it rather than to update it to 'beginners group' for consistency with other accounts of the period.

Frances became known around the world as 'John Stott's Secretary'. While the word 'secretary' would normally begin in the lower case, upper case appears when referring to Frances's job title. The term Study Assistant has been handled similarly.

'Whoever has my commands and obeys them,
he is the one who loves me.
He who loves me will be loved by my Father,
and I too will love him and show myself to him.'

John 14:21

Timeline

1925 Born 27 March at Bovey Tracey, Devon

1932 Older sister Pamela dies of leukaemia

1936 Leaves home for boarding school

1938 Begins at Malvern Girls' College

1943 Begins work at Radar Research and Development Establishment (RRDE)

1944 Father dies unexpectedly

1945 Moves to London after war ends

1947 Leaves UK for Switzerland

1949 Moves to South Africa

1951 Returns to England; settles in London and starts work at the BBC

1953 Professes faith in Christ, 1 January, at All Souls watch-night service

1954 Counsellor and supervisor in Billy Graham's Harringay Crusade

1956 Joins the staff of All Souls Church

1958 All Souls Clubhouse opens; *Basic Christianity* published (the first book Frances typed)

1960 Administrator for Church of England Evangelical Council (CEEC), constituted as first member of Evangelical Fellowship in the Anglican Communion (EFAC)

1970 Moves into downstairs office as Michael Baughen becomes Vicar of All Souls; administrator for new Langham Trust

1971 Administrator of new Evangelical Literature Trust (ELT); and appointed to new committee to oversee Langham Scholars programme

1973 Mother moves back to UK permanently. Purchase of home in Bourne End

1978 Happy Triumvirate is established

1982 London Institute for Contemporary Christianity opens

1996 Appointed to new group of John Stott's Literary Executors

2001 Awarded Lambeth MA. Late that year, Langham Partnership is founded, embracing ELT, Langham Scholars and Langham Preaching

2002 Evelyn Whitehead dies, aged 104

2004 Participates in BBC Radio 4 *Sunday Worship* recorded at The Hookses

2006 Celebratory lunch to mark 50 years of service as John Stott's Secretary

2007 Drives John Stott to College of St Barnabas

2011 Formal retirement from Langham Partnership (but not as John Stott's Secretary); and from John Stott's Literary Executors (remaining as a Consultant); John Stott dies, 27 July; participates in BBC Radio 4 *Sunday Worship* (broadcast 1 January 2012)

2012 Gives opening tribute at Memorial Service in St Paul's Cathedral, 13 January; places archives in Lambeth Palace; finally retires to Bourne End, Buckinghamshire

2014 Back in All Souls for the launch of *John Stott's Right Hand*, 21 September

2015 Celebrates her 90th birthday, 27 March

2019 Dies at her home in Bourne End, 1 June. Cremation service in Amersham, 20 June; Thanksgiving Service in All Souls, 21 June. Burial of ashes in Bovey Tracey, 1 July

Author's Preface

From the 1980s I enjoyed sporadic contact with Frances Whitehead, as hundreds of others had done, to ask for her help in arranging time with John Stott, or a contribution from him for a book or a magazine I was handling. Then, when on the staff of the Lausanne Movement, I found myself in touch more often.

Following Frances's eventual retirement in 2012, it was a pleasure to sit in the sun room at her home in Bourne End, looking out over the garden, and to share conversation, fellowship and laughter, interrupted often by sightings of swooping red kites. For she retained her childhood love of the natural world, first instilled by her father. 'The red kites,' Frances said, 'remind me of John. Once we spent a whole day looking for them in the Preseli Mountains, and didn't see a single one.'

The idea of writing Frances Whitehead's biography came from Pieter Kwant in 2013, when he listened to the interview with her on Mark Meynell's *Querentia* blog. I am glad she agreed to it, as it is a story which needs to be preserved. Midway through my writing, I learned from Rose McIlrath, Frances's oldest friend, of a conversation several years earlier with John Stott, in which he expressed his own hope that such a book should appear. We trust it will add a measure of completion to the biographies on John Stott, and to the doctoral theses already published on the nature, and the colossal influence, of his ministry.

Stott's ability to achieve so much, under God, could be described in human terms as the fruit of two factors: his self-discipline on the one hand; and Frances Whitehead's commitment to his vision, and her sheer capacity for hard work, on the other. For more than five decades they worked closely, first as a team of two, and later joined by a line of Study Assistants. Through their long and close working partnership they became good friends.

What was it in Frances Whitehead's character and personality that brought the drive, the exacting standards, the dominant streak, the occasional imperious tone, the tigerish protection, the pastoral concern, the warmth and laughter, and the doggedness, all mixed together? As for all of us, there are clues to our make-up in our family history. So to set the story of this unique partnership in its longer context of God's providence, you will find, while unusual for a book, an 'Interlude'. Here the reader is invited to glimpse a sweep of colourful history: on the Whitehead side from the mid-eighteenth century, and on the (maternal) Eastley side from the early-seventeenth century.

I have not attempted a full account of Frances's work as John Stott's Secretary. Indeed to do that would require a comprehensive account of John Stott's own work over that time. For to grasp the pressures, and indeed the essence, of Frances Whitehead's workload, we need to understand Stott's own work; his goals; networking; friendships; calling.[1]

How this book is shaped

The story is divided into five parts, each different in structure.

Part I opens with a single event in central London, the Memorial Service for John Stott, held in St Paul's Cathedral in January 2012.

Part II traces the chronological thread of Frances's life from her birth in 1925 to the early months of 1956, when she sensed that a move from her role in the BBC was likely.

Part III forms the *Interlude* described above, bringing a change of pace and mode.

Part IV reflects the fifty-five year story for which Frances Whitehead will be best remembered. The chapters in this section – which forms much of the book – do not move chronologically, as the strands of Frances Whitehead's responsibilities from 1956 soon become too diverse to be followed easily in a simple narrative. Instead, I have selected a few aspects of her role, and a few individuals with whom Frances worked, to give readers a broad feel; and I have given full chapters on their own to The Hookses (Stott's writing retreat for fifty years) and to the Masters degree awarded to Frances by the Archbishop of Canterbury.

Part V is given to Frances's final years, up to the burial of her ashes with her sister and father in Bovey Tracey.

This is followed by an Afterword with a reflection on the legacy John Stott and Frances Whitehead have left.

In several places the story of Frances Whitehead's life is carried through anecdotes and reminiscences. Let these reflections from a handful of friends stand to represent many more stories which could be told by others. I'm grateful to all those who have given time to help me build a picture of her life from others' perspectives.

Readers may reasonably ask why so much space is given in Frances Whitehead's biography to John Stott's life. The first answer is that Frances's ministry and his could not be pulled apart; the second is that Frances was keen for accuracy in the telling of John Stott's story, and within a short time of his death, inaccurate accounts had appeared. I offer this on my own behalf, and on Frances Whitehead's behalf, as authoritative material. It is the only published record to my knowledge, thus far, of the last few years of John Stott's life. So while not presented as an academic text, it may become useful for researchers, as it is drawn from primary sources. Each chapter of the first edition was approved by Frances as the book was shaped, and subsequent material by Rose McIlrath who knew Frances well for more than fifty years, and whom Frances named as her next of kin.

While I spent much time with Frances over recent years, and enjoyed her friendship, I have tried to maintain an objectivity, insofar as I could. At a personal level, I was particularly grateful for Frances's kind interest, as indeed for John's own, in my evangelical publishing ventures. In her final months Frances would urge me to 'get a move on' with a book I had begun to write in a rather different vein, but which sadly wasn't completed until after she died. This was about my cat, whom Frances had grandly named Simeon, after Charles Simeon of Cambridge, when he first arrived in 2013. Frances was enjoying episodes from the story as the chapters took shape.[2] She had a gift of moving from the spiritual and the serious to the funny, without trivialising the spiritual.

I want to record my gratitude to Bishop Timothy Dudley-Smith for providing the Introduction and to Chris Wright for his Foreword; both witnessed Frances Whitehead's contribution to the global Church from unique vantage points. I am indebted, too, to each of the people who appear in the book for sharing memories. In addition, I am grateful to the staff of All Souls and to several of Frances's friends who have helped me track down dates and details (any errors are mine and not theirs); to Karen Hegarty, Rebecca Rees and my sister Fiona Shoshan, for perceptive comments and questions as the initial manuscript took shape; and to Tania Loke and Jon Chan for their help in producing this updated edition.

JEMC
Oxford, June 2014
Updated March 2020

Foreword to the First Edition

Frances must have known about me for quite some time before I got to know her. Having heard John Stott often as a student in the late 1960s, I first met him in person in 1978 at the National Evangelical Conference on Social Ethics. With my newly-minted doctorate in the economic ethics of the Old Testament, I had been asked to give one of the Bible expositions. From then on John Stott (the convenor of the conference) took an interest in the career my wife Liz and I were then embarking on, in ordained pastoral ministry, theological teaching, and international mission. That involved a measure of correspondence between John and us over the ensuing years – correspondence which, from John's end, Frances must have typed. Doubtless I was one among several hundred names in her address book and filing cabinet . . . In those days 'Frances Whitehead' was a phenomenon one heard about but never saw, but whose existence was manifestly evident in John Stott's phenomenal output.

When Liz and I returned from five years in India in 1988, John invited me to be a trustee of the Evangelical Literature Trust. That meant regular board meetings in the basement of 12 Weymouth Street, entrance to which was by way of Frances' office. And Frances herself was one of the trustees and secretary. So I got to meet this 'phenomenon' more regularly. There was always a lovely warmth of welcome for all of us at those meetings. But I recall how over the decade or so that followed, the welcomes became more demonstrative – as the earlier formality gave way to ever more embracing hugs (from both of them) and a kiss (from Frances). For two such quintessentially unique individuals, with such backgrounds and life-stories, their capacity for genuinely loving and interested friendship was astonishing. In John's case it could be fostered by international travel and face-to-face meetings. For Frances, it all happened from a small office in central London, yet from there she participated in the global embrace of John's friendships.

What strikes me most, as I read Julia Cameron's beautifully-crafted biography of Frances, is the awesome providential sovereignty of God. Here were two individuals, with some similarities in their background and upbringing in England between the first and second world wars, one very urban and the other deeply rural – quite unknown to each other. Two people with very different life experiences and mixtures of personality traits, gifts, interests, and competences. And yet, by a series of what might look like co-incidences, or random choices (a lunchtime walk; a visit to an art-gallery), God engineered their coming together into a working partnership in which the gifts and energies of both could be fully deployed – serving each other in multiple human and hum-drum matters, and serving God's mission in their generation. It was a partnership in ministry with the gracious and sovereign hand of God on its origins, its operations, and its outcomes.

Church history will record the name of John Stott till the Lord returns. But the story of John Stott would have been very different, and simply could not have been what, by God's grace, it became, without the complementary ministry of Frances Whitehead – the lady behind the legend. John never wanted to be known as anything more than a humble servant of God. Neither does Frances. Every Bible reader knows Jeremiah, while few know about Baruch, his secretary. Baruch was a servant of the servant of the Lord. That was the role that Frances gave her life to fulfil. It was, as she says, 'a life, not a job'. Yet even Baruch has a small chapter to himself in the big book that carries the prophet's name. So in the midst of the many books by John Stott and about John Stott, it is altogether right and worthy that there should be one book dedicated to the woman who served her Lord by serving him.

Chris Wright
International Ministries Director
Langham Partnership

Introduction to the First Edition

Biographies are by no means always welcome. A. E. Houseman resolutely refused Assistance to a would-be biographer. Robert Bridges, Poet-Laureate, destroyed much of his personal archive, to frustrate any future attempts to write his *Life*. The problem can become even more acute if the subject is still alive when the book appears. Robert Runcie, Archbishop of Canterbury, was so dismayed by what his biographer had recounted, that he famously wrote to the author: 'I have done my best to die before this book is published. It now seems possible that I may not succeed.' When I was asked to write John Stott's Life, by his Advisory Group of Elders, I naturally consulted him about it. He firmly hoped that it would be for posthumous publication, and only as the work proceeded was he persuaded to change his mind. His reason for disliking the proposal was all to do with his characteristic humility, his rooted dislike – one could say almost fear – of self-aggrandisement. He cited to me, with distaste, celebrity autobiographies with titles like *Ego* or *Dear Me*. It is not a groundless misgiving. Even in the autobiography of so staid a man as Anthony Trollope, the words *I, me, my, myself* appear fifty times on a single page.

It seems safe to assume that the name of John Stott will already be known to readers of this book. Whether this is so or not, much of who he was, and of a life spent ('poured out' might be a more descriptive phrase) in the service of his Master, Jesus Christ, is to be found in the pages that follow. They also contain a description of Dr Billy Graham's first major Greater London Crusade at Harringay in 1954, in which John Stott played a significant part, and of the lifelong friendship forged between the two men. I remember having to make a train journey on the morning after the opening night of the Crusade, and avidly buying up a selection of newspapers at the station bookstall, to read the press accounts. Paper after paper carried the story on the front page – not normally given to anything 'religious' – and Billy Graham's name was in every headline. That railway journey came to my mind when I heard Billy Graham, on some later occasion, raise the question of whether there would be newspapers in heaven. It was not a very serious supposition, but it was to make a serious point. 'If there are newspapers in heaven,' he told his audience, 'it won't be my name that is in the headlines.' By the values of the world, the values of the Kingdom of Heaven will always seem topsy-turvy, as Jesus had to explain to his disciples at that Last Supper.

It would be no surprise to find that many readers who know the names of John Stott and Billy Graham know little, if anything, of Frances Whitehead, who is the subject of this book. I like to think that if there should be a *New Jerusalem Daily Press*, the names of Billy Graham and John Stott would indeed be in the headlines, and 'Frances Whitehead' up there beside them. I do not need to elaborate this, for all that follows in these pages makes crystal clear that John Stott could not have achieved the work he did without Frances at his elbow.

You will read, quite early on, of her conversion to Christ, for which her younger days were to leave her not unprepared. By the age of eighteen she had known two close bereavements; she must also be one of the last generation to learn the outline of her faith from the Catechism in the Prayer Book! From secret work in the war as a young mathematician, she came in the providence of God to work for the BBC, just across the street from All Souls Church, which was to become the centre, not just of her work, but of her life, for the rest of her days. Support for John Stott, as she looked back on it, was indeed 'a life, not a job'. But this Introduction is not really the place to cherry-pick incidents and episodes from that job and life. For that, you will want to move quickly on into Julia Cameron's thoroughly-researched account, from an insider's privileged viewpoint, in the chapters that follow.

But you must allow me to endorse, from my own experience, all that Julia writes and all that she quotes from John Stott, from his Study Assistants – indeed from all who knew Frances – of her gifts, pastoral and personal, as well as financial, administrative, editorial. In everything that touched John Stott and his work, she was enabler, supporter, adviser, encourager, as well as – to borrow terms from the media – gatekeeper and anchorman. With Frances in control, no-one was going to disturb John Stott's prayerfully planned programme without due cause; and any crisis that might dare to raise its head would quickly and resolutely be resolved.

This book, therefore, is much more than a personal tribute. It is that, of course. The late Penelope Fitzgerald, biographer and Booker prize novelist, gave it as her opinion that novels should be about those whom you think are sadly mistaken, but that 'you should write biographies of those you admire and respect.' This is clearly such a work. But it is also an important addition to the history of a period in which the evangelical stewardship of the gospel was undergoing expansion and renewal, written from the perspective of those involved. It is this which makes this biography a shining exception to the opening sentence of this Introduction. Later in the book you can read of how, when All Souls Rectory was a bachelor establishment of curates, students and other residents, some wag combined the words 'Rectory' and 'Vicarage' to name it 'The Wreckage'. It would have been better to combine them another way, so that all who lived and worked there in the days of John Stott and Frances were sharers in 'The Victory'!

Timothy Dudley-Smith
Ford, Wiltshire

'The Archangel in charge of postings'

Around the time of Frances Whitehead's appointment as John Stott's Secretary in 1956, Stott was approached by the Board of what is now the London School of Theology, to become its Principal. He would receive several approaches as the years passed, from the UK and beyond; from academia and the church. When the first such invitation came, an older friend wrote to say: 'If I were the Archangel in charge of postings, I should leave that said Rector where he is as long as possible.'[3] The Archangel did indeed leave John Stott there, but he did more. For he had been tracking the young woman who came to London in 1951, aged twenty-six; a woman with a fine mind and an unusual capacity for hard work, not yet a committed Christian, but for whom God had a particular calling.

John Stott's death was announced on the BBC news ticker, and his UK press obituaries commanded more space than would normally be given to a serving cabinet minister.[4] Many tributes appeared on social media and thirty thanksgiving services were held across the continents. Stott's impact was such that in April 2005, *TIME* magazine named him as one of the '100 most influential people' in the world. Under God he had exercised this ministry with barely any support staff. Without, as John called her, 'Frances the omnicompetent', such effective work on a range of fronts at once would not have been possible.

Frances Whitehead's story will now be told.

PART I

London. Friday 13 January, 2012

CHAPTER ONE

Memorial Service at St Paul's Cathedral

It was a cold, bright morning in central London. Around 9.30am, as rush-hour traffic was still moving very slowly, Frances Whitehead, aged 86, elegantly dressed in a mid-blue suit, got off a bus in Fleet Street, deciding instead to walk the remaining short distance over Ludgate Circus and up Ludgate Hill to St Paul's Cathedral. The occasion was the Memorial Service for John Stott, who had died on 27 July 2011.[5] In her bag was a finely-honed script.

Frances was accompanied by Mark Labberton, one of John Stott's former Study Assistants. They passed the City Thameslink Station on their right, with the Old Bailey off to the left. From the top of the hill they could see that hundreds of people had already begun to arrive and were queuing outside the Cathedral; it was clear that the seating would be full to capacity. Eighteen hundred places had been booked online very quickly after they were made available; a further two hundred had been kept back for people queuing on the day. The queues were abuzz with conversations and reunions.

St Paul's Cathedral is where John Stott aged twenty-four, having just finished at Cambridge, was ordained in December 1945. He was then about to begin his ministry as assistant curate at All Souls Church, Langham Place, in London's West End. He had grown up in Harley Street, the son of a thoracic consultant, and from his early years, he and his younger sister were taken to All Souls Church by their nanny. His earliest memory of the All Souls Rectory at 12 Weymouth Street, where he himself would later live for over fifty years, was of his Sunday school days in the mid 1920s, when he spent more time outside the classroom than inside it, excluded for terrorizing the girls with his toy guns and plastic daggers. A very different John Stott would emerge twenty years later as he stood in this great Cathedral to take serious and weighty ordination vows.

It was in the mid 1950s, as a young Rector, that he invited Frances Whitehead, a member of the congregation, to become his secretary. As history will bear witness, it would be hard now to imagine John without Frances; 'Uncle John' without 'Auntie Frances', as they became known. On this January morning in 2012, at the Memorial Service for one of the 20th century giants of the faith, Frances Whitehead, at John Stott's stated request, would give the opening tribute.

When Frances and Mark reached the Cathedral, they went straight in and joined others for Frances to have the usual voice checks at the microphone. Those taking part had seats reserved for them on the front row, beneath the dome. At 10.45am, the Cathedral staff opened the huge doors. People gradually filled the building, showing their entrance tickets, printed out at home like boarding passes. As they continued down the aisle in the long nave, everyone was handed the Order of Service. It showed John Stott's face in silhouette on the cover, illustrating a clear connection between him and his 'mentor', the great Charles Simeon of Cambridge.[6] As the line moved down the aisle, virgers[7] ushered people to seats, first filling the rows beneath the huge dome and gradually working backwards to the West door.

No stoles. No mitres.

There was a sense of reverence, of thankfulness, and of awe at Christopher Wren's marvellous imagination, and at the beauty of craftsmanship brought to its execution. For those who had watched the wedding of Prince Charles and Diana Spencer on television, or the Queen's 80th birthday and Diamond Jubilee, the striking black and white floor with its stark starburst mosaic under the dome held a strange familiarity.

What aesthetic richness in the stately Corinthian pillars, intricate artwork, and massive memorials; and for those who looked up, in the gloriously-painted dome ceiling, depicting scenes from the life of St Paul. Few looked up for very long. For, for all the grandeur of the setting, and formality of the occasion, there was no sense of stuffiness. Here was an historic gathering of friends from around the world; there was news to share, there were questions to ask, and greetings to be sent to people too frail to attend. Those taking part soon left their seats on the front row to greet old friends. Then, as the start of the service drew close, the All Souls Orchestra began to play, filling the Cathedral with works by Handel, Elgar, and Guilmant. Frances once more took her seat, next to Jane Williams, the wife of the Archbishop of Canterbury.

The congregation rose to sing the Processional hymn: Charles Wesley's 'Jesus! The Name high over all' to the tune *Lydia*. This exaltation of Christ, expressing a deep desire for wholehearted service of Christ, had been chosen by John Stott years earlier.

> *Jesus! The Name high over all*
> *In hell or earth or sky;*
> *Angels and men before it fall*
> *And devils fear and fly.*

The Procession made its way slowly down the aisle. As the hymn concluded, the Archbishops of Canterbury and York, and the Bishop of London were standing beneath the dome, facing the congregation. Something was different; something was missing, yet it took a moment to realize what it was. Here were the most senior Archbishops in the worldwide Anglican Communion, at a service in one of the best-known Cathedrals in the world. Yet they were not dressed in their usual ecclesiastical regalia; they were dressed in plain convocation robes. There were no stoles; no mitres; and the two Archbishops carried no crooks. This was surely out of honour for an evangelical statesman who never sought high office.

The Revd Canon Mark Oakley, Canon in Residence of the Cathedral, read the Bidding:

> 'We remember with joy and thanksgiving the life of John Robert Walmsley Stott, a minister of the gospel, beloved pastor, Bible scholar, mentor and friend. His simple life of study and prayer, preaching, writing and discipling, helped shape the face of a

twentieth-century evangelical faith in Britain and around the world. He was valiant for truth, even when that was unfashionable. John eschewed public accolades and ecclesiastical preferment and would be embarrassed by any service that dwelt on him or his achievements rather than pointing to his Saviour, crucified, risen, and ascended.'

The sheer dimensions, and the formality, of St Paul's Cathedral require a range of staff and servers. Wandsmen – servers dressed in robes and bearing wands – come to collect those who are about to address the congregation, and then lead them back to their seats afterwards. A wandsman duly came to collect Frances. Led by the wandsman, Frances approached the lectern when the Bidding Prayer ended. Michael Baughen, who had succeeded Stott as Rector of All Souls in 1975, introduced the tributes. 'Frances Whitehead', he said 'knew John better than almost anyone.'

Frances Whitehead's opening tribute

Those knowing the inner workings of John Stott's office in Weymouth Street had a shrewd sense of Frances's part in his ministry, but there were doubtless many in the Cathedral that morning who did not know. This in itself bore testimony to the spirit she brought to her role. Pressing her fine gifts into service, to enable John to serve Christ more effectively, she became a major means of multiplying his ministry. He could rely on her, and he did rely on her.

Frances laid her notes on the lectern and looked up. She spoke with authority, winsomeness, and clarity. Few indeed could have known John Stott as well as she did:

> Many tributes from all over the world have already been paid to John Stott. So I have asked myself what could I say that has not already been said, by way of gratitude to God for John's life. As for me, I know nothing but thankfulness for John himself, for his godly example, his concern for others regardless of race, colour or creed, and his faithful biblical preaching through which the light of Christ had first dawned on me.

Because I worked alongside him as his secretary for 55 years, perhaps I more than anybody can testify to the fact that, in his case, familiarity, far from breeding contempt, bred the very opposite – a deep respect, and one which inspired faith in the one true God. The more I observed his life and shared it with him, the more I appreciated the genuineness of his faith in Christ, so evident in his consuming passion for the glory of God, and his desire to conform his own life to the will of God. It was an authentic faith that fashioned his life – it gave him a servant heart and a deep compassion for all those in need, one that moved him to keep looking for ways in which he might be of encouragement and support to others, sharing his friendship and his own resources.

To work with John was to watch a hard-working man of great discipline and self-denial, but at the same time to see a life full of grace and warmth. His standards were high and he took trouble over all that he did; nothing was ever slapdash. He was consistent in every way and always kept his word. Although so gifted himself, he never made me feel inferior or unimportant. Instead, he would share and discuss his thoughts and plans with his Study Assistant and me, listening to our contributions, and eager to ensure consensus between the three of us – the 'happy triumvirate' as he would call us. So I found him easy to please and ever grateful for one's service.

The Scriptures lay at the heart of all John's teaching and preaching. His ability to interpret them was not simply a matter of the intellect, but of a heart full of love for Christ, and a longing to serve him faithfully, no matter what the cost in human terms. For he believed and submitted himself to the sovereignty of God and the Lordship of Christ in his own life – and he accepted the authority of the Bible as the word of God, regardless of ridicule by some.

Indeed, John taught and practised what he believed, and I thank God for the way he pointed me constantly to Jesus. 'Don't look at me,' he would say. 'Look at Jesus and listen to him.' But he also demonstrated the truth of what he was saying by his own example of obedience. This was the powerful magnet that drew people to put their faith in Christ as the Son of God and Saviour of the world. He believed that Christ lived on earth, died on the cross for our salvation, and will come again one day in glory. He believed that death is not the end, and that there will be a new creation in which we may all share, through repentance and faith in Jesus.

Thank God that John deeply believed all these truths, lived in the light of them, and maintained them, right to the very end. John's life was a wonderful example of what it means to be a true Christian – and what a blessing he was to all those who were privileged to know him.

As Frances Whitehead attested, John Stott 'deeply believed all these truths, right to the very end'. The Rugby schoolboy, converted to Christ aged seventeen, had finished well. Frances picked up her script and stepped away from the microphone. Her place at the lectern was taken by the Most Revd John Chew, Archbishop of South East Asia.[8]

Called, chosen and faithful

Not surprisingly, given the centrality of scripture in his ministry, Stott had wanted the Bible to be clearly handled in the Memorial service. His choice of a preacher was one of his oldest friends, the hymnwriter Timothy Dudley-Smith.[9] The sermon was based on Revelation 17:14 'Jesus is Lord of lords and King of kings, and those with him are called and chosen and faithful.' Eyes were directed to the risen, glorified Christ, and the sermon finished with a question often posed by John Stott as he concluded an address. Having laid out the historic facts of the gospel record, and a clear apologetic for its credibility, he would land his talk on the personal level, in a way which demanded a personal response. The Bishop did the same, finishing with Stott's familiar question: 'How is it between *you* and Jesus Christ?'

The service closed with Timothy Dudley-Smith's much-loved hymn 'Lord, for the Years'. Noel Tredinnick once more raised his baton and the All Souls Orchestra played the introduction as the congregation stood. With conviction, two thousand voices sang:

> *Lord, for the years your love has kept and guided,*
> *Urged and inspired us, cheered us on our way,*
> *Sought us and saved us, pardoned and provided,*
> *Lord of the years, we bring our thanks today.*

Frances had spoken of John Stott's integrity and consistency, and of his self-discipline and his obedience. His life was an example to follow; for like the Apostle Paul, John followed Christ's example. The final verse of the hymn summed up the prayerful aspiration of all as the service drew to a close:

> *Lord, for ourselves; in living power remake us,*
> *Self on the cross and Christ upon the throne;*
> *Past put behind us, for the future take us,*
> *Lord of our lives, to live for Christ alone.*

The congregation sat or kneeled as the Archbishop of York and the Bishop of London led the final prayers, then the Archbishop of Canterbury pronounced the blessing. As these senior leaders of the Church of England processed out, one wondered if they would ever be seen again together, wearing such little emblem of high ecclesiastical office.

PART II

From Childhood to the BBC
(1925-1956)

CHAPTER TWO
Early years: 1925-1936

Frances Whitehead's father, Captain Claude Maguire Whitehead DSO MC, returned from the Great War seriously injured, having had his left shoulder blown away.[10] He had been educated at Repton, then at Clare College, Cambridge. From here he gained a mining qualification in Sheffield before sailing to South Africa, where close relatives lived; here he became underground manager at the Robinson Deep Gold Mine in Johannesburg. Claude Whitehead happened to be back in England on holiday when war was declared in 1914, and immediately joined up as a trooper, receiving a commission soon afterwards. The Whitehead family suffered severe loss in his generation; both of Claude's younger brothers died within a matter of weeks on the Somme.

Frances's mother, Evelyn Eastley, grew up in Paignton, Devon, where the Whitehead family also lived. Evelyn nursed Claude Whitehead after he came home. Before the war, she had been in love with his younger brother Hugh, so it was natural for her to be drawn into the grieving process of the family as she worked through her own grief. While Claude and Evelyn were very different in age – he sixteen years her senior – and in temperament, the circumstances of life drew them together and they became engaged in 1922; a year later they were married.

Claude and Evelyn purchased a small country home with a walled garden, an orchard and several fields, at the foot of Beara Cleave, near the village of Bovey Tracey in South Devon. The village dated back to Saxon times. A house had stood on the site of the Whiteheads' home since the eleventh century, and its name, Beara, appeared in the Domesday Book.

On their first Christmas, Claude gave Evelyn a bound volume of the Book of Common Prayer with Hymns Ancient and Modern. He wrote in the front: 'To Darling Bobs with love from Claude, Christmas 1923' adding the final verse of his favourite hymn, John Keble's 'New every morning is the Love':

> *Only, O Lord, in thy dear love*
> *Fit us for perfect rest above;*
> *And help us this and every day*
> *To live more nearly as we pray.*

He evidently had a sense of God, and a reverence for him in daily life.

Arrival of two daughters and Pamela's tragic illness

Two months later, on 22 February 1924, their first daughter, Pamela, was born; and on 27 March 1925 Frances arrived, named after her paternal great grandmother, the illustrious Frances Maguire. (See Interlude.) Family photographs from the 1920s show two little girls, similarly dressed, playing with family pets and clutching favourite toys. But tragedy befell the family when Pamela reached six or seven years old, as she was diagnosed with leukaemia. By the time little Frances was old enough to play games with her older sister, Pamela was spending much time in bed. As the doctors' visits increased, and a live-in nurse was needed, Frances was sent to stay with one or other of her grandmothers. It was a lonely existence; partly as there were no other children to play with; and partly as Frances longed to be with her sister, whose illness seemed to be shrouded in mystery, to protect Frances from anxiety. Pamela died in the spring of 1932, shortly after her eighth birthday, when Frances was not quite seven years old.

The fields beyond Beara's garden gave onto rising woodland, which in the springtime was blanketed in primroses. Frances and her parents picked hundreds upon hundreds of these, and wove them into a cross, to lay on Pamela's coffin. She was buried in the Bovey cemetery.

Anxiety over Pamela's illness had taken a deep toll, and Evelyn's mother urged that the family go on holiday, to rest and be refreshed. So not long after Pamela's death, Frances sailed with her parents to Madeira. On board ship, Frances's mother got to know a fellow traveller, Sylvia Dunsford, who became drawn into the family's company. Sylvia, like Evelyn, had lost her fiancé in the war, and the two women formed a deep bond. This new friendship would soon re-shape family life.

Family life at Beara

Beara was a busy place. The Whiteheads grew much fruit produce – strawberries, raspberries, gooseberries, blackcurrants, apples, from which Frances's mother made many jars of jam and apple jelly in a shed behind the house, fitted with a large paraffin stove. She worked hard, selling produce to local shops and in nearby Newton Abbott. Claude Whitehead kept several hives of bees, from which honeycomb was extracted and sold, and oversaw the vegetable garden with a huge asparagus bed, all grown for the same local shops.

A wedding present to Claude and Evelyn from an Eastley cousin had taken the form of a breeding pair of Old English sheepdogs, an added hobby for Claude. In due course half a dozen kennels housed these dogs, some sold, others shown, and several won championships at Crufts.[11] Pamela and Frances had learned to walk by clinging onto them. Claude also kept Rhode Island Reds, by then a popular breed of hen, for eggs and for flavoursome meat.

Two further additions were made to the Beara animal community when the family returned from Madeira. Frances's Uncle William, who owned Welstor Farm up on Dartmoor, gave Frances a Shetland pony with a foal to look after, to help take her mind off her sadness at the loss of her sister. Now new daily routines began as Frances learned how to care for her new friends, and learned to ride. As the foal was broken in, there were tossings-off and bruises, but Frances was not easily beaten and the foal was gradually mastered. She would ride her pony to the blacksmith in Bovey Tracey to be shod, watching the sizzle on each hoof as its shoes were fitted. From this point in her life, Frances would adopt a keen interest in horses and in the equestrian world.

The family employed two staff, Mortimer the gardener, and his wife who helped in the kitchen. However, Evelyn's mother became concerned that Evelyn was too pressured, given the amount of work needing to be done in the home and garden. So, within a short time of returning from Madeira, the Whiteheads engaged two Swiss au pairs to help ease the load.

The death of a child is always an enormous test for a marriage. Evelyn naturally wanted to talk about Pamela, but Claude mourned silently and deeply and did not want her name mentioned. Amid the activity of Beara life, tensions between Evelyn and Claude, two very different people, were soon to surface; however they took care not to argue in front of Frances.

It was around this time that Captain Whitehead and Evelyn first turned their minds to Frances's formal education, deciding to hire a governess. This decision served to extend Frances's rather solitary existence, as she had no children to play with. She recalls her governess cycling to Beara on an old pedal bike; a woman probably in her forties, whom the young girl perceived as 'very old'.

One of the downstairs sitting rooms was designated as the schoolroom, and here Frances applied herself to her lessons. Claude Whitehead had already taught his daughter to write with the help of a copy book, where, as was the practice for decades, children copied row upon row of a single letter; then rows of another letter. Claude had also taught her to read. So, when the governess arrived, he continued, not surprisingly, to retain a keen and active interest in Frances's tutoring, and to complement it out of class-time. It was a particular frustration to Captain Whitehead that the method of teaching algebra had changed over one generation, and his systems and those of the governess were not in accord.

As well as mastering 'the three Rs', Frances learned to play the piano on the family's baby grand. In addition, her parents wanted her to develop skills in arts and craft. Her father had a gift for painting and for sketching, and Pamela had shown early signs of artistic ability. So two sisters came regularly to teach Frances these skills. But she had no aptitude for art; indeed she never got past the stage of covering a cardboard box in fancy wrapping paper.

Claude Whitehead loved games of every kind. He was a good sportsman, and had competed as a hurdler at Cambridge. Despite his war injury, he continued to play golf with a handicap of par, and he and Evelyn were both active in the local tennis club, as well as playing on their own hard court at Beara.

Frances's father was devoted to Frances and took her with him whenever he was going out. At the age of eight he gave her an air rifle and taught her to shoot at a bulls-eye set up on the lawn. From here she graduated to taking pot shots at birds. By the age of nine she was handling a two-bore shotgun with cartridges, and shooting rabbits in the fields, which her Pekinese dog would run to retrieve. She and her father would sometimes go off rabbiting together in the woods accompanied by Mortimer, sending ferrets down the holes to chase out the rabbits. When Frances's shots were not quite on target, Mortimer would finish the task. Claude loved the natural world and was widely knowledgeable. He would encourage Frances to identify flora and fauna, to listen to the birdsong and distinguish the bird species. He himself belonged to a pheasant shoot, went fishing, and was a good horseman, despite his war injury.

Father and daughter played endless card games at home too, of which Bezique was a favourite. These games would start straight after breakfast, before the Governess arrived, much to Evelyn's disapproval. Claude Whitehead's streak of fun and love of games and puzzles delighted his daughter; a trait she herself would retain.

Frances's father was evidently viewed as a kindly man, for in the years following the Great War, ex-soldiers, former members of his regiment, used to track him down, and come to Beara to ask for money and help.

Claude Whitehead took Frances with him each Sunday to the local Anglican church, where, to a child, the services seemed formal and a little arid. Her father, who evidently had a personal faith which mattered to him, would insist every week that she learn the Collect[12] for the day by heart. Before he kissed Frances goodnight, he would sit with her while she said her prayers, always including the Lord's Prayer; this she would race through. 'Girlie, STOP!' he would often exclaim. 'You haven't thought about a *single* word you've said.' In the same manner, Frances learned the Questions and Answers of the Catechism in the Book of Common Prayer, again schooled by her father.

After two years of being tutored at home, it was time to send Frances to school. Rather than sending her to the village school, her parents enrolled her in a small private school in Bovey with just six pupils. Her father drove her there each day. On summer afternoons she and her father would watch cricket in the field opposite the school before driving home. Claude Whitehead drove a roomy Fiat with a canvas hood, which he would pull back in good weather. But by the time Frances was ten, there was a new daily pattern. Instead, they would travel to and from school in the second family car, an Austin Seven. It was at this young age that Frances now learned to drive. Each afternoon, as soon as Captain Whitehead turned off the main road from the village and into the lane leading up to Beara, he and Frances would get out of the car and change places. Kangaroo starts and crashing gears would, over the weeks, give way to smooth gear changes, and another skill mastered.

Her parents' separation was now in the offing, but Frances's mother resolved to remain at Beara until Frances left for boarding school at the age of eleven.

CHAPTER THREE
To Boarding School: 1936-1943

September 1936. Frances and her parents packed her school trunk, and her father heaved it into the Fiat. Excitement and anticipation were mixed with uncertainties. As for any child leaving home for boarding school, there were many different emotions. For Frances this moment marked a watershed in all aspects of life. For in addition to a new school, new friends, and dorm life, the landscape at home was changing. Her mother would now be leaving Beara to live with her friend Sylvia Dunsford, whom she had met on board ship as the family sailed to Madeira four years earlier.

Lanherne School in Dawlish, on the south coast, was just twelve or thirteen miles away. After her rather solitary life at home since Pamela's illness became serious, Frances was glad to have the company of girls her own age. She had inherited her father's love of fun and of sport and enjoyed the camaraderie of boarding school life, as well as the chance to compete in tennis and netball.

Each day would begin with a service in the chapel for the whole school, after which a long crocodile of girls in green uniform would process along the Promenade, back to the main building. Continuing her father's work ethic, and wanting to please him, Frances always aimed to be the best, in sport and in the classroom.

Following a sports injury at Lanherne, she found herself unable to play sport for several weeks. For those excluded from games lessons, a special curriculum was devised. This consisted mainly of scripture, and focused almost exclusively on lessons from the Old Testament, in particular Kings and Chronicles. This was, as far as Frances could remember, the first time she had read the Bible herself. It would however be another twenty years before she grasped how the Bible storyline fitted together.

While Frances was still young, her mother would often return to Beara for school holidays, sometimes accompanied by her friend Sylvia. It was an unusual arrangement, but made to work. Claude and Evelyn Whitehead never divorced. When Evelyn was back home, she would take Frances to Sunday worship at the ancient church of St John the Baptist in the village of Lustleigh, a few miles north of Bovey. Frances found the services more friendly than those in the Bovey Tracey Parish church of St John the Evangelist, which her father continued to attend. The vicar in Lustleigh struck Frances as a humble, gentle, kindly sort of person, and the service was lower-church in its style. It was the personality of the vicar and the warmth of his preaching which made them want to keep going back.

To Malvern

At the age of thirteen, in 1938, Frances was sent to Malvern Girls' College in the spa town of Great Malvern, Worcestershire. The Belfast-born writer and Christian apologist C S Lewis had also received his schooling in the town, a quarter of a century earlier, at the boys' school, Malvern College.

Malvern Girls' College, founded towards the end of the nineteenth century, was situated in the Imperial Hotel, opposite the railway station. The girls were a familiar sight to townspeople with their heather-coloured tweed overcoats and maroon hats. By the time Frances entered the school, Miss Iris Brookes had been Headmistress for ten years. She was a controversial figure from the start of her tenure, and evidently commanded authority, not only over the staff and pupils, but, by virtue of her redoubtable presence, over the Town Council. According to Pamela Hurdle, the school's historian, there was a sense in which she resembled Muriel Spark's character – or Maggie Smith's screen interpretation of it, in *The Prime of Miss Jean Brodie*. In the first year of her appointment, and in response to her criticism, the Council reduced its rather inflated attendance allowance at meetings, settling for a modest sum and 'the democratic third class railway fare'. Should a steam train in the station make enough noise to disturb the headmistress, a member of staff would be dispatched across the road to seek out the station master, and the noise was subdued. 'Her standards must have been difficult to meet,' stated the school historian, 'One girl seeking a reference from Miss Brooks was told that she could not make bricks without straw, while another girl quietly doing some non-examination work was told to give up and switch off the light since it was not worth using the electricity for her efforts.'[13]

Summerside House

The Middle School was divided into six Houses, all situated in nearby roads. Here girls from Lower IVth to Upper Vth ate breakfast and dinner together. Frances was in Summerside House, in North Albert Road, just a few minutes' walk from the main school building, where the senior girls lived. Each morning the Summerside girls would assemble in a crocodile, to walk down to the main building, supervised by prefects, returning together in late afternoon, when they could change out of their uniforms and into their home clothes. In summer, the tweed coats were exchanged for plain blue blazers, or, when seniors, stripy blazers of red, white and blue.

After a year, war came, and the buildings were requisitioned by the Royal Navy. At this point the school was relocated to Somerset, and split up by year groups. Frances's year moved to a mansion house in Hinton St George with several staff. However, the evacuation lasted only one year, before they moved back to Malvern, as the Navy had not needed the buildings.

A particular aim of public schools[14] has always been that of nurturing confidence and poise. To this end, Miss Brookes had introduced a custom whereby all girls, from the age of thirteen, were required to deliver a three-minute speech to their whole house each term, with the Housemistress present. No instruction was given on how to choose a subject or on how to craft a speech; and the girls were not appraised for their efforts. Frances tended to speak on horses or riding, and no doubt marshalled good content. But she, like many others, dreaded the delivery, and she was able to enjoy term only when this ordeal was over. She was probably not the only girl who left school vowing never again to speak in public.

Girls were required to write to their parents weekly. Frances always knew there would be a letter from her father, as Captain Whitehead wrote weekly to his daughter. Other girls' fathers hardly ever wrote, and they envied Frances her letters from her father. Her mother wrote too, but not as regularly. Her father's letters were full of encouragement to be the best, and expressed his high expectations. If anything was worth doing – study, sports or the pursuit of interests in school clubs – it was worth doing well. Her father instilled in Frances that she must always aim high. Claude Whitehead continued to retain a close interest in his daughter's education, as he had when she was under a governess.

As with all public schools, the chaplain prepared pupils for confirmation in the Church of England. Other than those from a different Christian tradition, all the girls were confirmed, in Malvern Priory, by the Bishop of Worcester. Wartime travel restrictions meant Frances's father was unable to be there, but her mother made it, as did a few other parents; the confirmation candidates, all dressed in white, knelt at the communion rail, one by one receiving the Bishop's blessing. For such schoolgirls this was more a rite of passage than a public confession of faith; and so it was for Frances.

It became second nature to work hard at everything. At Malvern Frances attained Grade 8 at the piano and, in middle school, she would accompany the hymn-singing in house prayers. Having begun piano lessons when very young, Frances's love of music, particularly classical music – Schubert, Chopin, Bach, Mozart, Beethoven – was to last throughout her life.

Sport also continued to play a big part in her life until it was crowded out by work. Frances competed for Summerside and for the school, in tennis, and also played lacrosse. She loved the rivalry of sports, and the fun of piling into coaches for away games. Malvern life contrasted so starkly with life at Bovey Tracey.

In her Vth form, Frances was made a prefect, and appointed Head of Summerside House, a role involving some discipline of younger girls, supervisory duties, and arranging walks for Sunday afternoons. She was evidently showing both leadership and administrative gifts. In her oversight of the girls she worked to reflect the values instilled by her father. He urged her to be honest about what she had done at all times, and never to tell untruths, no matter how bad the situation seemed.

The eleven commandments

From the time Evelyn left home, Claude Whitehead would take Frances with him to bridge parties in the school holidays. It was a natural progression for him, as he wanted her to learn his wide range of skills. In addition Claude and Frances began to go up to Welstor Farm after church each week, for Sunday lunch with her cousins. Frances would drive the Austin Seven from Beara to the main road, as was now customary, and then take the wheel again when they were up on Dartmoor, as soon as they turned off the road into the half-mile-long drive up to the farmhouse.

Welstor, one of several farms owned by the Whitley family, had a large, old-fashioned farmhouse, and other houses on its land. Frances's Uncle William was Master of the South Devon foxhounds, and a keen huntsman. Frances, a competent horsewoman from her early teens, would join the foxhunt. The family had wide interests in the natural world and in history. Frances's Aunt Nonnie (her father's sister) was a keen collector of flint stone-age arrowheads to be found among early settlers on Dartmoor.

William Whitley was highly-regarded in the county, both as a landowner, and for an unusual initiative he took in 1928. As a staunch Anglican, he was troubled by what he considered 'a popish trend' in a new Book of Common Prayer to be introduced. Stanley Baldwin's government rejected this, to his relief. To mark this outcome, Frances's Uncle commissioned a well-known sculptor, W A Clement, to engrave the Ten Commandments on two 'tablets of stone', two adjacent rock faces which lay up at Buckland Beacon, just above Welstor; this was a major undertaking on a very exposed promontory. The work, now a local landmark, was completed on 31 August that year.

As some space on the stones remained, Clement suggested that Mr Whitley might like to add an eleventh commandment, which he did. So the Ten Commandments end with John 13:34 'A new commandment I give unto you, That ye love one another, as I have loved you, that ye also love one another' and the engraving is completed by a verse from the hymn 'O God, our help in ages past'.

The closeness Frances shared with her father was precious to both of them, and she always remembered him with deep affection. Shortly after leaving school, unexpected tragedy would bring an end to her Beara days, and to this special bond.

CHAPTER FOUR
Massive changes: 1943-1947

Frances left Malvern Girls' College aged eighteen, in the summer of 1943, and immediately joined the war effort. Her first job was in Malvern Link, in the Radar Research and Development Establishment (RRDE). Here she was one of a team of thirty men and women.

Part of their work was to investigate what lay behind 'anomalous propagation', that is, the way searchlights perform differently according to weather conditions and pressure in the atmosphere. This information, gained through simulators, provided a 'reasonable expectation' on how effective searchlights would be in differing weather patterns.

The data collected would be used in deciding how and when the allies should send out their aircraft. Surprise was obviously a critical element in air raids. This data from simulated sources gave the RAF the best guess on the extent to which cloud cover would hide aircrafts; further, it showed how far distant their own craft needed to remain, to fly undetected by enemy radar.

Frances, who excelled in maths, was designated to the team's Mathematics Department, acting essentially as a human computer. She would be given equations with different variables, and, with the help of a slide-rule, plot points on a graph.

Frances's father wrote weekly, responding to news he received from Frances, updating her on local happenings, and often mentioning what he had been reading. His letter of 21 January 1944 opened with his usual fond greeting 'My Darling old girl'. Claude Whitehead was the local Commander of Special Constables, and halfway through the letter, he explained how he had been called out three days earlier at about 8pm, to investigate a reported light in Bovey. He wrote:

> 'I thought I had just enough petrol to get me into Bovey and back. I found no light, and coming back my car stopped at the bottom of Atway and I found I had run out of petrol!! I knew one of my special patrols was coming along, so I just waited for them, and with the help of another man we pushed the car up the hill into the lane and left it there for the night. What a game! It took some pushing up the hill.'

Then he closed with news of high winds. While the incident was relayed in a 'by the way' fashion, Claude must have been in significant discomfort as the strenuous effort in pushing the car uphill had caused his heart to move two-and-a-half inches. A few weeks later, as he was still unwell, Frances sought compassionate leave, and special permission to travel, which was granted. Her father was delighted at the prospect of seeing her, but there is still no trace in his letter of the seriousness of his situation.

'Darling old girl' he wrote on 16 March, 'How delightful to think of seeing you on Saturday, but am afraid you are getting a wangler!' He told her that a car had been arranged to meet her at Newton Abbot station on the mainline, and she would need to look out for the driver.

On the morning of Saturday 18 March, Frances made her way to Malvern station to take a 10.30am train down to the West Country, looking forward to seeing her father. When she reached Newton Abbot she found unexpectedly that her aunt was there to meet her.

How's Daddy?

'How's Daddy?' asked Frances as soon as they were both in the car. She could barely take in her aunt's words. Her beloved father, suffering from a coronary thrombosis, had died earlier that afternoon. Having no indication from his letters of his condition being serious, let alone terminal, this news came as a profound and terrible shock. Frances arrived in Beara to find her father laid out, surrounded by candles, in the room in which she had received her first lessons from a governess. She felt totally desolate.

Her mother, by then engaged in war work and living in Leamington Spa, arrived the following day, and the funeral took place in Bovey Tracey Parish Church. Claude was buried alongside Pamela in the local cemetery. In the numbness of the days following, Frances found it hard to grasp that Beara would have to be sold. This proved another painful loss.

It was decided that Frances and her father's sister, her Auntie Dolly, would both live at Welstor Farm, in one of its houses. Frances would use this as a base for holidays, while continuing in her job in Malvern. The farm had been a second home for years, enjoyed with her father, and her double bereavement of losing him and also losing Beara brought deep pangs of sorrow. While Frances had several cousins in the Whitley family, they were much older than she. Their kinship nonetheless brought some comfort.

Everything in Frances's life had changed, just a few days before her nineteenth birthday. Her father's death and the new somewhat makeshift arrangements in Welstor gave a deep sense of rootlessness. While Frances returned to Welstor as her new base for several years, it was all so different from the security she had known up to then, with Claude Whitehead acting as father and mother, a rock in her young life.

Colleagues at the RRDE, sensing something of her devastation in losing her father, showed kindness. As a way of giving her a break, she was sent to Cambridge for two weeks, to work at the Cavendish Laboratory, then under the direction of the Nobel laureate, Sir Lawrence Bragg. Wartime Cambridge, which escaped bombing, remained much as it had been before the war, affording few concessions to the nation's new realities, at least on a superficial level, beyond the appointing by each college of its Air Raid Precaution (ARP) volunteers. Frances stayed in the Garden House Hotel, situated within easy reach of the Cavendish Laboratory, where she was set to work entering data into its huge computer. The hotel offered a welcome change for a fortnight from her not-very-comfortable digs in Malvern, which she shared with a fellow Malvernian also working at the RRDE. Here the young women had only a small baby Belling on which to cook, and mice could be seen running up the curtains.

A move to Lambeth

As the war finished, Frances's role at the RRDE came to an end. While wondering what lay ahead, she accompanied her mother on a short holiday in the New Forest. Here she went out riding every day. During the week, she found herself riding in the company of Oliver Gibbs-Smith, who served as both vicar of St John's Wood and the Archdeacon of London. As they talked, Frances spoke of her desire for a change, perhaps a move to London. Oliver Gibbs-Smith put her in touch with an architect friend in the Ministry of Works, Colonel Tweddell, whom he knew was looking for a secretary.

Frances had received some secretarial training in her final year at school, and was offered a job in the Ministry of Works, based in Lambeth on the South Bank of the Thames. The Ministry had been formed in 1943 originally to handle property requisitioned for use in the war; then in the post-war years it carried responsibility for government building projects. The construction of thousands of new homes, to replace those which had been bombed, was a pressing need, nowhere more so than in London, where the housing stock was seriously depleted. In 1945 a new surge of building began. In the UK over 150,000 prefabricated homes – flats, terraces, semi-detached houses – were constructed, mostly in London. They could be erected in comparatively few man-hours without dependence on bricks, and proved a popular temporary solution to housing needs. The first block of flats in London, functional and pleasantly-designed, was opened by the Minister of Works in February 1946. While prefabs were intended as a stop-gap solution for families, some were to remain for decades, and a few into the new century.

From this point onwards, Frances returned less frequently to Devon, and found a bedsit near Earls Court, in West London. Frances's mother and Sylvia Dunsford were by now living in Ardingly, a picturesque village thirty miles south of London, in West Sussex. Frances would go and stay with them, and their Alsatian dog, Carlo, at weekends. In due course, further change would come, in a direction Frances could not have anticipated.

CHAPTER FIVE
Switzerland and Cape Town: 1947-1951

The early years of peace-time brought immense relief to everyone. For many it would mean a gradual path through the 1950s to home ownership and to slowly-greater prosperity. For those who had lost loved ones, there would be massive personal adjustment. As life returned to a new semblance of normality, Evelyn and Sylvia, instead of resuming a comfortable life in Britain, decided in 1947 to move overseas.

Sylvia Dunsford had cousins living in Switzerland who suggested to them that they should move there. The idea appealed to Evelyn as she had spent a year at a Swiss Finishing School and had loved it, so they decided to settle in Montreux, on Lake Geneva, where Sylvia's relations lived. At their invitation, Frances, now aged twenty-one, decided to leave her job in London and to go with them. The house in Ardingly was duly sold, and Evelyn and Sylvia found a spacious flat overlooking the Chateau de Chillon.

It was not an easy time for Frances, who was still grieving the loss of her father. She had no work permit so enrolled at the town's School of Languages, and was glad to use time to improve her French. Under-employed, and with the rawness of bereavement, her days hung heavily, even depressingly. Frances played tennis, learned to ski, and took Carlo the Alsatian for walks in the local woods. While a couple of boyfriends at different times lifted her spirits, her life overall seemed empty; she felt she was drifting and she missed her father's counsel.

Two years after arriving in Switzerland, in 1949, more change would come. Through Sylvia's cousins, Sylvia, Evelyn and Frances had got to know a husband and wife from South Africa, with whom they spent much time. In talking with them a new idea surfaced, that of another international move. Evelyn and Sylvia were persuaded to explore a move to South Africa, with a view to purchasing a sugar cane farm in Natal, and employing a manager to run it. The prospect sounded very attractive.

Such a venture would require financial assistance from Evelyn's mother, back in Paignton. Beatrice Eastley was surprised at the plan and sensed it had been Sylvia Dunsford's idea. But Evelyn's voice tended to be the dominant voice when it came to moving, and it was her wanderlust which would take them out of Europe. Having to leave Carlo behind, with a Swiss maid, was a painful loss for all three women. The Alsatian had been a faithful friend.

They travelled by train to Venice, where they boarded a boat to Durban, sailing through the Suez Canal. Having no particular guidance on where to settle, they travelled first up to Zululand. The terrain and the culture were not easy for westerners. Frances's father had grown up in South Africa, and would have returned to the Johannesburg goldmine if he had not been injured in the war, and met Evelyn Eastley in his convalescence. But Evelyn had no experience of the country, and she, Sylvia and Frances learned as they went. On one occasion they were told a black mamba snake had wound its way under their car. This is the fastest and longest snake on the continent, and its venom the deadliest.

They were advised to travel down to Cape Town, where they first took a flat in the Oranjezicht area. Then for a short while they lived on a snake farm belonging to people with whom Sylvia and Evelyn had fallen into conversation as they travelled. An unusual setting indeed for such women, but the travelling trio needed somewhere to stay while they searched for a farm to buy, and accommodation was available here. The snakes were kept in pits, where they were bred so they could be 'milked' for venom, which would then be used to counter the venom in those who had received snake bites. It was a very different kind of life from Beara days.

A fruit farm in Paarl

In due course Evelyn Whitehead and Sylvia Dunsford learned of a fruit farm which would soon be for sale in Dal Josafat, near Paarl, in Western Cape Province, thirty-five miles northeast of Cape Town. Paarl was the third-oldest town in South Africa, after Cape Town and Stellenbosch, following the arrival of the European settlers. The area is known for its scenic beauty and its fruit-growing heritage. It would become the focus of international news in February 1990, when Nelson Mandela completed the last days of his prison sentence in the Victor Verster Correctional Centre, where he was given a house. It was from Paarl that the last straight of the nation's journey began, to achieve multi-racial elections, and to abandon apartheid.

The farmhouse into which the women then moved was situated just below the home of John Russell, the Marquess of Tavistock and future 13th Duke of Bedford, who arrived there to farm a year or two earlier. (On succeeding his father as Duke of Bedford, he would later court much controversy by opening Woburn Abbey, the Bedford family seat, to the public, and introducing a safari park to its grounds.) The water supply, piped downhill from a dam above the Russells' home, was shared by both households; the Russells' needs taking priority because they were higher up the hillside.

There was no proper sanitation, and the lavatory was a simple hole in the ground in an out-house. There was no mains electricity – just oil lamps. Farming was a new world to these women, but within a few months some simple houses had been built for black farmworkers and servants, and a manager appointed. The orchards grew figs, apricots and guavas, while buchu, a herbal tea introduced to South Africa by the Dutch colonists, grew on the hillside. In addition there was a vineyard. The household kept a cow, a mule, and also Susie, another Alsatian, but no dog could really replace Carlo.

There was consternation one day when the cow became bloated and lay down in her stall, distressed in her breathing. Frances sat down beside her, and supported the recumbent cow's head in her lap as they waited for the vet to arrive, uncertain whether the cow would survive. In due course the vet arrived, treated the cow, and the cow rapidly recovered. This story was to endear Frances to Rose McIlrath, a veterinary surgeon, whom she met a few years later, and who was to become a lifelong friend.

Frances helped in the orchards when the fruit was ripe, and drove crates of fruit into Cape Town each week to sell in the market. In due course she came to the point where she wanted a job away from home. Soon, to her own surprise, she found herself living in Constancia, on the north side of Table Mountain, helping to look after five small children, including a four-month-old baby. Never having held a baby before, she was not a natural nanny. Frances made friends with fellow nannies in the area as they took children for walks, and she enjoyed going on holiday with the family; but she longed for greater purpose.

Back in Paarl, she sat one day in the vineyard weeping. She was conscious of civil unrest in South Africa, and the injustice of apartheid, issues from which she had been shielded in Devon and in Malvern. She was concerned by the political climate and the supremacy of the whites in the apartheid regime. Over these years she began to develop a social conscience. But there were deeper issues, ones which she could not define. Why was she so unhappy in such a beautiful place?

She felt she was simply marking time. The countryside was stunning and yet she could not appreciate it. She felt lonely, unsettled, and struggled to make sense of life. There was nothing to aim for. In school she had worked hard for exams, and worked to get into the first sports teams. Her father had always urged her on. But here she sensed no goal in her life, and no one to help her find direction.

In 1951, Frances's grandmother came out to stay. When it was time for Beatrice Eastley to return home, Frances was asked to accompany her back to Devon, to save her travelling alone. She was glad to do this, and as she boarded the ship, she wondered whether or not she would ever return to the Western Cape. Edgar, Frances's boyfriend from her days in Switzerland, had written to say he hoped to marry her, but Frances was less certain and wrote to decline. Perhaps she would stay in the UK; she was not sure.

The boat journey from Cape Town to Southampton took three weeks. On board ship Frances got to know Ian, a Rhodes scholar who was returning to Balliol College, Oxford for post-doctoral research. Ian had been raised a Roman Catholic but had no personal commitment to Catholicism or to Christ. As the days went by, the friendship turned to romance. In God's economy, while the relationship did not last, it was to have a special bearing on Frances's coming to faith in Christ.

CHAPTER SIX

London, the BBC and a new-found faith: 1951-1956

Britain was a very different Britain from the one Frances had left in 1947. The much-heralded Festival of Britain would run throughout the summer, to mark the centenary of Prince Albert's 1851 Great Exhibition. It was hoped that this would add a further spur to redevelopment and to morale-boosting after the end of the Second World War. The Festival would capture the mood of the post-war nation, with millions now settling down in their new homes and new jobs. After all the wartime restrictions, and now with a little money to spend, people were planning visits to relatives, and days out.

For Frances, the thought of returning to the loneliness of life in South Africa, where she had wept on the hillside with a sense of purposelessness, held no attraction; she resolved that she would remain back in England, for the time being. Having made her decision to stay, at least through The Festival of Britain, she wrote to her mother. Evelyn knew how much Frances enjoyed the arts, and that life on the fruit farm did not provide much opportunity for aesthetic pursuits; she replied to Frances's letter to say she understood. After a few weeks spent in Devon with her grandmother, Frances was drawn back to life in London.

Frances needed to find a job. So, travelling up from Devon to London by train, to visit her friend Doreen from Malvern days, she scanned the columns in *The Times*. Here she saw an advertisement for a temporary secretary at the BBC, to work for a talks producer in the overseas service. This would provide a foothold for her without long-term commitment. She applied and was duly appointed. Her department was based at 200 Oxford Street, close to Oxford Circus. From London it would be easy to see more of Ian in Oxford, with the frequent and easy train service from Paddington. In God's providence, she never returned to South Africa. London would become home for the next sixty years.

Frances was able to share digs with her school friend at 66 Princes Square in Bayswater. Doreen, a gifted pianist and cellist some years her senior, was teaching music at a private school close to the Royal Albert Hall. They had become friends at Malvern, when Doreen had helped Frances with her piano playing. London offered rich cultural pursuits for the two women with their common love of music.

In due course, Frances was invited to apply for a permanent appointment at the BBC, working for a talks producer in the West Africa service who held a dual role. As well as creating educational programmes, she also produced talks in the Overseas Service (now the BBC World Service) for programmes on culture, with slots for book reviewers, concert critics and theatre critics. The interview for this dual role was with the formidable feminist, Mary Treadgold, literary editor and Carnegie medal winner. Here Frances fielded a completely unexpected question. 'You're not an evangelical, are you?' Frances, not yet a committed Christian, was unfamiliar with the term. She could have betrayed her puzzlement, but the tone of the producer's voice gave away her sheer distaste for evangelicals. 'Oh no!' said Frances. Obviously competent in all aspects the roles would require, she was appointed.

Frances discovers All Souls

A few months after she arrived at the BBC, news came that her department would be moved to new offices in the Langham Hotel, at the top of Upper Regent Street. She and a fellow secretary decided to walk up there one lunchtime, to look at their new quarters. Frances noticed that the doors were open at All Souls Church, which stands opposite the Langham Hotel and adjacent to Broadcasting House, the main BBC building, and she felt strangely drawn to look inside. This church, designed by John Nash and opened in 1824, is situated at the bend of the road, as Upper Regent Street turns into Portland Place. The building looks not unlike a rocket on its launching pad. With its curving steps and Corinthian pillars, it remains a well-known West End landmark. In December 1940, a landmine exploded in Portland Place, which brought down much of the church ceiling. The restoration work after the war took until April 1951, when the congregation was able to return. She found a light, modern church, so unlike those in Bovey or Lustleigh. A commanding painting by Richard Westall, *Ecce Homo* (Behold the Man), depicting Christ, bound and on trial, hung in the east end. This painting, clearly visible from the pavement, with spotlights shining on it, immediately drew Frances's attention.[15]

After the office relocated to the Langham Hotel, Frances was again drawn into All Souls, as, on her lunchtime walk one day, she noticed a concert with a string quartet was about to start, and so she went in and sat down. Not many people were there. The concert finished and Frances got up to leave. While she had appreciated the music, she felt disappointed at the lack of any sense of welcome. There seemed such a contrast between the welcome of the building, into which she had been drawn a few months earlier, and the indifference of the few people there. As she walked back to the office she resolved not to go again.

A few months later, Frances was taking her lunchtime walk with a particular spring in her step on a bright, sunny day. The BBC staff were often offered complimentary tickets to sundry events, and Frances had just received tickets to Lords cricket ground. She found her mind taken back to her schooldays, when she watched cricket with her father on the green in Bovey Tracey. As she walked through central London, she could hear church bells ringing from the tower of St Peter's Church in Vere Street, a narrow street off Oxford Street, running along the side of Debenhams. St Peter's was a sister church of All Souls, under the oversight of its young Rector. It was here that the Sunday services had been held after the damage was caused to All Souls by the wartime landmine, and here that a weekly lunchtime service now took place.

Frances was intrigued to hear bells in the middle of the week, and decided to go inside the church to investigate. Within a few minutes the small building filled up with office workers, shop assistants and shoppers. Timing was everything for the success of a lunchtime meeting, as people needed to return to their desks promptly. Around 1.15pm the speaker stood up, tall, dark-haired, wearing a dog-collar and a dark double-breasted suit, with a Bible in his hand. Like Frances, he spoke with a cultured English accent. He was evidently the product of a public school. But it was not this which struck her. She had never heard anyone opening up the Bible like this. The young Rector took a passage of scripture, and explained its meaning with a deep sense of passion. He evidently believed everything he said, and he spoke with an unusual authority. Frances went back to the service the following week, and began to attend it regularly; when she found out that St Peter's was linked to All Souls, she started to go to All Souls on a Sunday too.

George Cansdale, Superintendent of the Zoological Society of London, and known to the British public as 'the Zoo man', was a churchwarden of All Souls. Frances had got to know him as he contributed to programmes on the BBC, and she would act on behalf of her boss, the producer, in supervising his talks. These were pre-recorded in a basement studio of Broadcasting House, against the gentle soundscape of one of London's underground rivers gurgling below. For Frances it was good to see a familiar face at church. As the months passed, she was regularly in All Souls, Sunday by Sunday, hearing the Bible opened up in a way which enthralled her.

All the while, Frances and Ian maintained their friendship across the fifty miles which lay between London and Oxford. On one visit to Oxford, Ian took Frances to the university's Ashmolean Museum, an imposing building in Beaumont Street, with its towering Corinthian columns. Ian showed Frances a painting which hung in the great central stairwell and which had evidently captured his imagination. Frances stood looking upwards at it, absorbed by what she saw, and by Ian's interest in it.[16] Here was Moses, standing in the wilderness, his arms raised high in the air, lifting up a serpent on a pole. Frances did not know the story it illustrated from scripture,[17] nor its dramatic foreshadowing of Christ being raised up on the cross, but the image stayed with her.

Midnight, as 1953 begins

All Souls held a watchnight service each New Year's Eve, and on 31 December 1952, Frances was there. John Stott, the Rector of All Souls, now thirty-one, was already becoming well-known for his preaching, and the church was full. Stott was an evangelist, and he chose his scripture reading from the third chapter of John's gospel. 'As Moses lifted up the serpent in the wilderness, so shall the Son of Man be lifted up.' Frances was listening closely. Could that be the inspiration for the painting Ian had shown her in the Ashmolean? Imagine her surprise when the Rector spoke of the painting in his sermon! Moses lifted up the serpent, and urged the Israelites to look at it, and be healed of the sickness from their snake bites. So Christ was lifted up on the cross, and we are invited to look up to him, and receive forgiveness for our sins. Slowly the truths were falling into place. Here was an ancient story, depicted in art, which bridged the gulf between God and Man. God had ordained that the Israelites would be healed by looking up at a serpent on a pole. That same God had ordained forgiveness for the whole world through Christ's death on a cross. That night, Frances Whitehead looked up to Christ, and found forgiveness, healing, meaning.

The sheer authenticity of the preacher had convinced Frances to listen and to focus. The Holy Spirit had, over the previous several months, brought home the truth of the words of scripture. Shortly after midnight as 1953 dawned, this young woman met with the living Christ. As the service closed, the Rector invited those who would like to echo a prayer of repentance, and of belief in Christ, to stay behind and hear more of the Christian life. Frances echoed the prayer, but felt too shy to join a small group gathering at the front of the church, so she left straight away and walked home.

Describing that night over sixty years later, Frances said, 'the presence of Christ was so vivid. It was a real encounter with the Lord

– with light; as real as though Christ himself was somehow shining in the church. It was extraordinary. I walked back to my digs with a tangible sense of his companionship. No one tried to pressure me or persuade me.' In the years since her father died, she had longed for direction, for purpose, for goals. Now she had a new reason for living: for Christ, who was lifted up on the cross, as Moses had lifted up the serpent in the wilderness.

Frances had learned from her father that there was a seriousness about spiritual things; she had yearned for a deeper meaning in life, yet been unable to find it in Switzerland or South Africa. The lunchtime services had awoken a new spiritual awareness. As the weeks went by, she had begun to feel a hypocrite, as she was reminded of her father's loving rebuke. 'GIRLIE, you haven't thought about a *single* word you've said. You're talking much too fast.' How many times, she wondered, had she prayed to God, 'Thy will be done'? What had it meant for her life? They had been no more than empty words.

Some months later, a letter arrived from Ian, to say he wanted to finish their relationship. For Frances this news was devastating, and she sat down and wept, feeling the pain of total rejection. Then something surprising happened. 'It was as though the Lord came, and there was light,' she said. It was just as she had experienced on New Year's morning: a deep and tangible sense of Christ's companionship.

◆ ◆ ◆

Frances Whitehead, twenty-eight years old, attractive, poised, well-educated, and having lived in three countries, would have had good reason to exude confidence. Her days as Head of Summerside House were not many years behind her, and she was carrying increasing responsibility at work. However, while regularly attending worship at All Souls on Sundays, and joining the midweek lunchtime service in St Peter's, Vere Street, a sense of diffidence was evident. She still didn't know others in church, and she was reticent to volunteer for anything. Six months after her profession of faith, she decided this must change.

One Sunday she saw there were forms which one could fill in, with a box indicating a desire to serve. Frances filled in a form, ticking the box.

It would be easier for her if someone from the church took the initiative, and made contact with her. Sure enough, she received a call from the Rector, inviting her to meet with him for fifteen minutes, in the inner vestry at All Souls, after work. When Frances arrived, he was dressed in his cassock, ready to address a gathering of the annual All Souls Bible School, which was about to start. John Stott wanted to get to know new church members himself, to ascertain how best to help them. It was immediately clear from their conversation that Frances did not yet understand much Christian truth; so while Frances had ticked the box to offer service, the question of how she could be used was not broached. As time was short, Stott scheduled a further meeting. The following week, after another brief conversation, he suggested to Frances that she join what was then called a 'nursery class' for new believers.

From here, Frances got to know church members, and over the months that followed she became deeply involved in All Souls activities. After joining the class, she met Joan Beresford, a church member who also worked in the BBC, and who invited her to the staff Christian Union. She went to the first meeting feeling shy and gauche, still bearing the marks of her solitary childhood. Here she was met by an American, Lorne Sanny, of the Navigators,[18] who had moved to London to help set up arrangements for Billy Graham's 1954 Harringay Crusade. Frances was struck by his humility as he put out chairs for the meeting at which he would be speaking. This soon became for Frances a fellowship in which she felt comfortable.

Through using Bible study notes from the Navigator movement, and with the Navigator emphasis on memorizing scripture, Frances began her lifelong daily habit of reading the Bible and praying. While cycling to and from the BBC each day, she would learn Bible verses by heart. Frances was invited to join the All Souls ten-week training course on Wednesday evenings to become a 'commissioned worker'. This course, which concluded with an exam and an interview with the Rector, took its members through central tenets of the faith, methods of evangelism, and how to apply scripture in daily life. In addition, all members had to commit to regular attendance at the fortnightly prayer meeting. At the end of the course, participants were assigned to roles which suited their gifts. For Frances this was to visit families whose children came to the weekly Family Service, held at St Peter's. This was not always an easy task, especially for Harley Street families, whose schedules did not easily accommodate such visits. She was also invited to co-lead a nursery class with Richard Bowdler, Chaplain to the stores in Oxford Street, which met each Friday lunchtime. Her earlier shyness was dissolving, and she was glad of the chance to explain Christian truth and to offer friendship to group members, most of whom were new to All Souls and some new to London.

Billy Graham at Harringay

Frances had been a committed Christian for a little over a year when the Harringay Crusade began, on 1 March 1954. It ran night after night for ten weeks. This event marked a watershed in the life of the American evangelist, for whom it was his first crusade outside the United States. John Stott and the All Souls congregation were deeply involved in it. Across London, no-one could miss the fact that the Crusade was happening. The whole nation was aware of it as Billy Graham featured on the front pages in the national press, and on Pathé News in the cinemas. The stadium was filled to its 11,000 capacity each evening with coaches arriving from towns and cities within a fifty-mile radius. Billy Graham also held rallies in Hyde Park and Trafalgar Square, addressed meetings in US military bases, and preached to the Queen in Windsor Chapel. On the final evening of the Crusade, 12 May 1954, the venue was instead Wembley Stadium. Its 120,000 seats were soon filled, as was the overflow, the 67,000-seat stadium in White City.

Each evening of those twelve weeks would conclude with what were to become very familiar words: 'Now I'm going to ask you to get up out of your seats and make your way down to the front. The coaches will wait.' Hundreds professed faith in Christ each night, pouring down the aisles, as the crowds sang the hymn 'Just as I am'. Stewards would direct each person to a trained counsellor.

Several hundred counsellors were needed over the twelve weeks, and they would catch the bus or tube to Harringay after work as often as they were able. The Crusade had already begun when Frances was drawn in to help as a Counsellor. While still young in the faith, she knew what she believed and could support it from scripture. One of Billy Graham's team, Irene Bailey from the US Navigators, gave her some training, and she joined the team, talking with those who had come forward, and passing information to her supervisor so they could be invited to a local church. Shortly after starting in this role, she became an Advisor to a group of Counsellors, ensuring that newcomers to the faith had their questions answered, and received suitable counsel.

It was around this time that Frances got to know Ann Bates, who served on the staff of Scripture Union, working in the Varsity and Public Schools (VPS) section, among girls in schools like Malvern. Frances's friend Doreen was soon to get married and leave Bayswater, and Ann, who had a flat in nearby Westbourne Terrace, was looking for a flatmate. She asked Frances if she would like to share with her. The VPS (pronounced Veeps) department arranged camps for senior schoolchildren in the Easter and summer vacations. These camps were begun by the Scripture Union evangelist E J H Nash (known as 'Bash') and they focused on teaching the Bible, and teaching leadership skills. John Stott, who was converted to Christ while a schoolboy at Rugby, had been drawn into these camps himself in 1938.[19]

Frances was a member of the BBC Riding Club. Once a week after work they hired horses from the civil service stables in Victoria, and rode up to the barracks of the household cavalry in Knightsbridge, under the instruction of a sergeant major. Frances's love of riding led Ann to invite her to join the Officer team that summer at a VPS riding camp, held at Kingham Hill School in the Cotswolds. This brought Frances into another aspect of Christian ministry, as she got to know the girls in her assigned dormitory.

While Frances was enjoying new friendships made through the BBC and All Souls, and through meeting Ann's friends, she was at the same time beginning to feel unsettled. She wondered whether she should explore a change, possibly going to Bible college. There was no discernible call to a particular ministry or a part of the world, but she wanted to be obedient, if Christ wanted her to serve overseas. So she asked for a meeting with the Rector, which was duly arranged for the following week, one day after work. She explained her willingness to leave the BBC and go to Bible college. He asked a few questions but did not sound very positive; he instead made what seemed a rather fatuous suggestion. She left the meeting feeling perhaps a little despondent, but then put it out of her mind.

PART III

Interlude

INTERLUDE

Snapshots from family history

Here we change mode, pace and direction. We will dip into family stories traced back to 1761 on the Whitehead side,[20] and to 1600 on the Eastley side. It is a family history of endeavour, privilege, deprivation, courage, and military honour. For Frances, it is a story of provenance and predilection, happiness and tragedy, all under the providence of God; for her background and circumstances had forged in her strengths and qualities she would draw on in her long commitment to Christ, and to the man whose work she would enable.

Maguire heritage

Frances's father, Claude Maguire Whitehead, carried in his middle name his Irish roots. The Maguires married into the English Whitehead family in 1827, when Frances Ann Maguire (1808-1901) married Henry Whitehead (1801-1874), so becoming the first Frances Whitehead, Frances's great grandmother.

This first Frances Whitehead was named after her father, Francis Maguire (1760-1811), a Surgeon-Major in the 4th King's Own Regiment of Foot, and her grandfather, Francis Maguire, the earliest known of that name, who owned a small estate in Cashel, County Tipperary. The first Frances Whitehead's illustrious mother, Elizabeth Maguire, née Houghton, ran away from home to get married at the age of fifteen. She was strong-minded and unusually gifted, with a doughty Irish spirit. Elizabeth's family never gave their blessing to the union, and ties were sadly severed. Over the years to come, she would often travel with her husband's regiment, even after the first children were born. Her life was neither easy nor safe.

Whitehead Genealogy

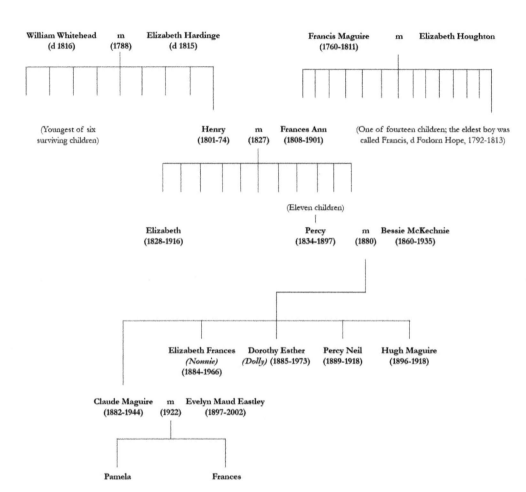

William Whitehead m Elizabeth Hardinge
(d 1816) (1788) (d 1815)

Francis Maguire m Elizabeth Houghton
(1760-1811)

(Youngest of six
surviving children)

Henry m Frances Ann
(1801-74) (1827) (1808-1901)

(One of fourteen children; the eldest boy was
called Francis, d Forlorn Hope, 1792-1813)

(Eleven children)

Elizabeth
(1828-1916)

Percy m Bessie McKechnie
(1834-1897) (1880) (1860-1935)

Elizabeth Frances
(Nonnie)
(1884-1966)

Dorothy Esther
(Dolly) (1885-1973)

Percy Neil
(1889-1918)

Hugh Maguire
(1896-1918)

Claude Maguire m Evelyn Maud Eastley
(1882-1944) (1922) (1897-2002)

Pamela

Frances

Eastley Genealogy

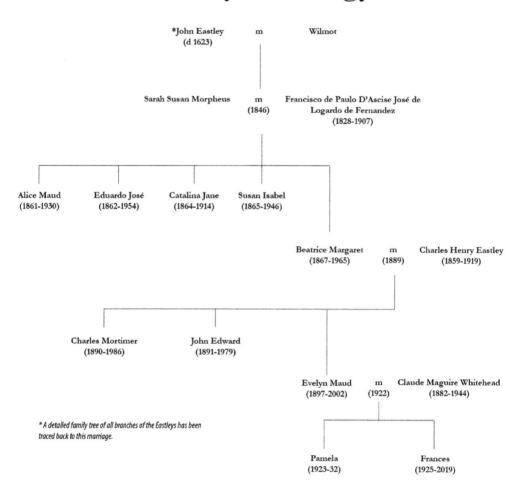

*John Eastley   m   Wilmot
(d 1623)

Sarah Susan Morpheus   m   Francisco de Paulo D'Ascise José de
(1846)   Logardo de Fernandez
(1828-1907)

Alice Maud   Eduardo José   Catalina Jane   Susan Isabel
(1861-1930)   (1862-1954)   (1864-1914)   (1865-1946)

Beatrice Margaret   m   Charles Henry Eastley
(1867-1965)   (1889)   (1859-1919)

Charles Mortimer   John Edward
(1890-1986)   (1891-1979)

Evelyn Maud   m   Claude Maguire Whitehead
(1897-2002)   (1922)   (1882-1944)

*A detailed family tree of all branches of the Eastleys has been
traced back to this marriage.

Pamela   Frances
(1923-32)   (1925-2019)

Mother and son rescue regimental colours

In 1797 as the regiment sailed home from Quebec (with young Francis aged almost five, and a younger brother) their vessels 'fell in with a French privateer *La Vengeance*, and after a running fight in which several men were wounded, they were overpowered and captured.' It was Mrs Maguire who saved the regimental colours from falling into French hands, wrapping them round her curling irons and dropping them through a portal into the sea. Towed into Brest Harbour, defeated, the several hundred prisoners were taken to the Castle and thrust into a single room. Mrs Maguire was the only woman among them. In cramped squalor, she would in due course give birth to her first daughter, with rats running over her bed, behind a makeshift screen of coats.

After a year of captivity, the Maguires broke free by riding concealed in a dung cart to a port, and they were finally able to return to their London home in Park Lane. Francis and Elizabeth Maguire had fourteen children, of whom only seven survived into adulthood. Francis, their eldest, evidently with his mother's doughty spirit, received a commission aged twelve and joined the regiment aged sixteen. His company was assaulted at Vittoria in Spain where he 'resolutely placed the regiment colours on the parapet, where they were shot to pieces in his hands.' He was killed on his twenty-first birthday, 31 August, 1813,[21] in 'the Forlorn Hope' as he led men in the siege of San Sebastian. We learn that his youngest brother, Tom Maguire, led a very different life. He married a daughter of the Sotheby family, art dealers, and died in 1895, aged ninety.

Whiteheads, attempted regicide, and London litterati

The Whitehead story begins in 1761, with the birth of William Whitehead, an enterprising young northerner who came to London to seek adventure. His parents were landowners on the Yorkshire / Lancashire border. No more is known of his family, but tradition has it that, after arguing with his parents, he left home with half a crown in his pocket, and arrived in London asleep, on the top of a hay cart, the last stage of his two-hundred-mile journey.[22] His story is the stuff of legends.

William next appears in family records as married to Elizabeth Hardinge from Hertfordshire, and living in Little Cadogan Place, Chelsea, as 'a successful contractor, builder and architect, and a much-respected Chelsea landowner'. In May 1800, aged thirty-nine, he and a friend were sitting in the stalls in Drury Lane Theatre. The performance was attended by King George III. Suddenly:

> 'a man beside them suddenly leapt to his feet and levelled a pistol at the King in the royal box. William Whitehead had only time to throw himself forward and wrench away the pistol which went off, the bullet smashing the chandelier in the roof.'[23]

William Whitehead was personally thanked by the King for saving his life, and offered a knighthood, which he modestly declined. Perhaps as a credit to his modesty, a different favour was bestowed on him. From that date he was appointed Master Architect and Royal Bricklayer, and given charge of the fabric of all the royal palaces. The vinery at Hampton Court stands as one of his several contributions to the royal properties.

Whitehead was a friend of the poet and playwright Richard Sheridan (1751-1816) whose finances wavered from riches to poverty. Sheridan achieved great success with *The Rivals*, and for some years owned Drury Lane Theatre. He moved in high society, and retained many prosperous friends even when his own fortunes declined, at which point he gained creditors, of whom Whitehead was one. Elizabeth Whitehead (later Elizabeth Malleson), the family chronicler, records wryly how, each time her grandfather went to remind Sheridan of his debt, 'he was entertained with such delightful talk and such amusing stories that he came away with his errand unaccomplished.'

William built Whitehead's Grove in Chelsea, moving into number 7, which became the family home for three generations. His wife Elizabeth died in 1815, and William a year later in 1816, aged only fifty-five. They left six surviving children (three had died in infancy), all well provided for. Much of William's estate consisted of land and houses. He evidently had foresight to see the wisdom of such investment. His memorial stone describes him as 'A man with an uncommon share of natural talent, unwearied zeal and inflexible industry in performing whatever he undertook' and referred to 'Many National Works which bear testimony to his skill as a Builder'.

William Whitehead commended the younger of his children into the care of the older ones. However, as his granddaughter records, 'None of his children, unhappily, seems to have inherited his enterprising spirit and business instincts, and their being left orphans so early contributed no doubt to their ineptitude and helplessness.'

Bailiffs and Prince Albert's buttons

Henry, the youngest Whitehead son, who was fifteen when his father died, became a solicitor, and built a lucrative practice in Chelsea. It was in 1827 that he married Frances Anne Maguire, the first Frances Whitehead. They moved into 7 Whitehead's Grove. It seems that he or his law firm was entrusted with oversight of much of the family's estate. While this would make sense from the family's perspective, it did not serve the family well.

Henry Whitehead had, as a young man, been on a 'grand tour' and was used to spending money. He kept a country home as well as his Chelsea town house, and he extended 7 Whitehead's Grove with a conservatory, storerooms, office space and stables for his horses. But behind the scenes his finances were precarious. Two factors were at play. *First*, his easy-going and generous temperament meant he cared more about others' affairs than his own. *Secondly*, he joined the Unitarian Church, a decision which lost his firm several major clients. This easy-going and kind nature meant he lent money which he did not retrieve, gave much time and expertise pro bono, and often paid bills for his less-monied friends. We read:

'Through inattention or want of business capacity, he allowed leaseholds to lapse and mortgages to go unredeemed. In this way he lost all the land lying east of Sloane Street, now 'the Gardens', and piece by piece his property slipped from his hands.'

Henry and Frances Whitehead had a strong marriage, which held together through these testing times. We learn that 'to find a bailiff ensconced in the Chelsea kitchen ceased to be a novelty'. Together with Chelsea ambivalence about Unitarians, his lack of care for business matters would in large part cause the loss of his family fortune. Frances took charge insofar as she was able and the family moved several times in efforts to keep expenditure down, sometimes letting 7 Whitehead's Grove and living either in the country or in a smaller house in New Burlington Street. Frances at one stage opened an embroidery business, and took on an assignment for the Royal Household to decorate Prince Albert's waistcoats.

Henry Whitehead died in Godalming and his widow Frances outlived him by twenty-seven years. In exchange for a small annuity, she gave one of her sons-in-law the last remaining property of William Whitehead's estate: a row of houses where Harrods now stands.

Frances's grandfather, Percy Whitehead

Elizabeth Whitehead, Henry Whitehead's eldest child, retained a particular affection for her youngest brother Percy (our Frances's grandfather) who left home in Whitehead's Grove aged sixteen, bound for New Zealand.[24]

Evidently a serious-minded youth, he wrote to his family asking to receive pamphlets written by John Stuart Mill (later a friend of Elizabeth) and works of Plato. 'The older I grow, the less do I care about light reading; but my desire to study the principles that regulate government, religion and morality increases', he wrote. Then in a letter in February 1865 he stated, 'If I ever have a son, he shall be taught grammar and logic.'

At first Percy Whitehead learned sheep farming. After several years of this in New Zealand, he sailed to South Africa where again he began by buying sheep. From his letters one learns of his immersion into wider South African life at a troubled time, petitioning over the railways, and strenuously rescuing the injured in war. Around the start of the first Boer War, he moved into mining, once more teaching himself a new discipline and finding his way around a new industry. It was in this period of his life, at the age of forty-five, that Percy Whitehead met Bessie McKechnie. She was of Scottish Presbyterian descent, and not yet twenty-one years old, but from the beginning of their friendship they both knew they wanted to marry. They married in 1880, and were to have three sons and two daughters. It was a happy marriage and the children grew up with a firm Christian understanding.

While Percy's early days of sheep farming had not created wealth, his mining company would create wealth. Percy died when in Johannesburg in 1897, aged sixty-two, owning a gold mining company, and a substantial property portfolio. By the time of Percy Whitehead's death, he and his family had moved back to the UK and had settled in Paignton, with Percy returning to South Africa as needed for business.

Their oldest child, Claude Maguire Whitehead, Frances's father, had intended to spend his career in the mining industry. But while he was on holiday, visiting his mother, the First World War was declared. So instead of returning to South Africa, he joined the armed forces, and would serve in Salonika with the second battalion of what was now the Royal King's Own Lancaster Regiment.[25] And thus the Whitehead scene was set for the curtain to rise at the beginning of our story.

The Eastleys of Devonshire

Charles Eastley, Frances's uncle on her mother's side, delved carefully into family history, with the central aim of establishing the correct Seal for the family to use.[26] So while personal stories and anecdotes have not been chronicled, we have a good record of lineage.

The Eastleys of Devonshire can be traced back over four hundred years, with various spellings of their name. For, as Charles Eastley observes, 'spelling did not count for much through the period of the Reformation, the Tudors and the Stuarts, the Roundheads and Royalists'. So as well as the spelling Eastley, there are records of Eastlight, Easlyght, Eastleighs, Easley and Eastly.

The family lived for at least seven generations as comfortable Yeomen, in a mansion house, Stantor, and farmed land in Marldon, a few miles west of Paignton. Eventually they would move into Paignton. Many of the family lie buried in the churchyards of the Marldon and Cockington churches, or under their tiled floors. Indeed when some scaffolding was erected in Marldon church in the early 1960s, it went through the floor, and thereby uncovered a large tomb of Eastley graves.

An early 17th century Will includes a gift of ten shillings 'for the poor of Marldon, to remain to the use of them forever', twenty shillings to one daughter, £5 to another; £10 to a son, 12d to each grandchild, and the entire residue to another son. One can only wonder at the reactions of siblings at the reading of the Will.

The Spanish connection

Frances's maternal grandfather, Charles Henry Eastley, was a solicitor in Paignton, following in a line of Eastley solicitors from the mid-18th century. He died on his sixtieth birthday, in 1919. He and his wife, Beatrice, had three children: Charles, who joined the family law firm, John, who practised law in Bombay, and Evelyn, Frances's mother.

Beatrice Eastley was the daughter of the splendidly-named Spaniard, Francisco de Paulo D'Ascise Jose de Logardo de Fernandez (1828-1907). Francisco de Fernandez, Frances's great-grandfather, was educated in England where to his parents' displeasure he became a Protestant, and in their eyes a heretic. As a young man, he had to escape Spain as a stowaway under gunfire. He managed to reach England, trained in medicine and surgery, and served with the British Army in India and Hong Kong, China, and Crimea. In the Crimea he performed surgery in a rudimentary operating theatre, assisted by Florence Nightingale; they scrubbed up for surgery by washing their hands in a china bowl, later brought to England, which Fernandez had acquired in the Orient.

Frances's grandmother died in Paignton at the age of ninety-eight in 1965. She had outlived her husband by over forty-five years. Longevity evidently runs in the women's line of the family.

The Singer connection

Major clients in the Eastley law practice in Paignton were the Singer family, whose father Isaac Merritt Singer had founded the international sewing machine company. Isaac Singer had courted much controversy, having sired eighteen children by a wife and mistresses in the US, before moving to Europe and marrying again in 1863. His new family, with six more children, was eventually to settle in Oldway Mansion in Paignton. His third son, Paris, renovated one of its facades to make it look like the Palace of Versailles.

Charles Eastley's law firm looked after the affairs of the Singer family for decades, hence their appearance in this family's life. The Singers had enormous wealth, some of which was used for benevolence to the community. They were generous to the Eastleys, but were viewed within the family with a measure of ambivalence. Beatrice Eastley, Frances's grandmother, regarded them with some disdain as nouveau riche. Sharp disagreement on whether the family should continue to handle the Singers' affairs would appear in the next generation.

There was no question of dishonesty or malpractice in the Singer family. Indeed Paris Singer and Mortimer Singer were well-known for their philanthropy. But the opulence of Singer life, and the large income from their account, seemed to demand a hold on the Eastleys, and led to many arguments. The discomfort caused by this colourful family, for whatever reason, blighted the Eastleys, leaving a permanent rift in the family. Frances's uncle, Charles Eastley, joined the family firm. But John Eastley, just a year younger, and also a lawyer, instead went to India, and practised in Bombay.

When Frances's parents were married in Paignton, Evelyn Eastley, with her mother Beatrice's support, resolved not to invite any of the Singers to the wedding. It is often wryly joked that weddings are the most expensive ways of offending people. But this omission in the guest list must have taken particular courage from Evelyn, knowing it would cause acute embarrassment to her brother Charles, and her late father's colleagues. It sent an unambiguous message.

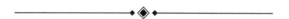

So we arrive in Paignton at the end of the Great War, with Claude Whitehead, a wounded officer, and Evelyn Eastley, a bereaved fiancée; and with Frances's grandmothers living within half a mile of each other.

As we now turn to Frances Whitehead's fifty-five years as John Stott's Secretary, this background may provide some insights into her make-up, some reasons for facets of her character, her values, and her personality: the exacting standards, the dominant streak, the occasional imperious tone, the patience and the impatience, the austerity, the fierce protection of time, the doggedness, never separated far from pastoral concern, warmth, and laughter.

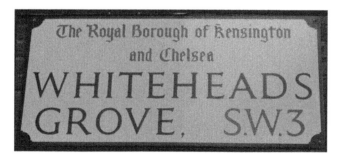

The family home at number 7 no longer stands.

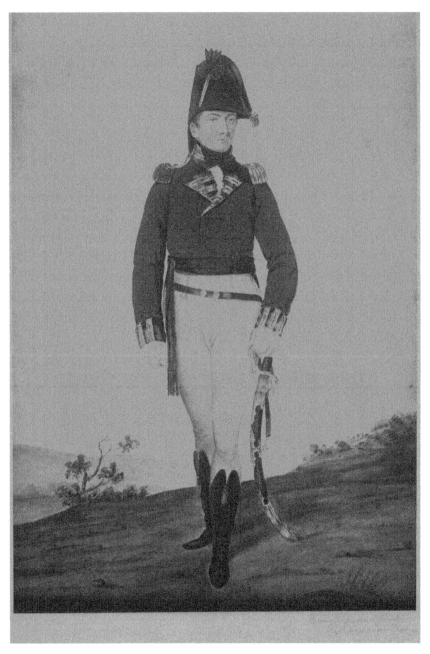

Lieutenant Francis Maguire, who died on his 21st birthday in 1813.

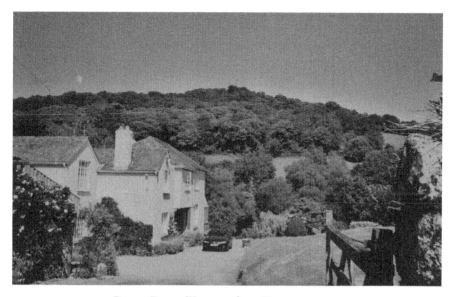

Beara, Bovey Tracey, where Frances grew up.

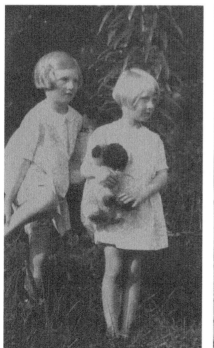 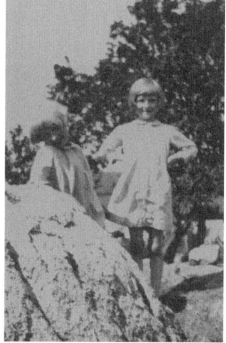

Frances with her older sister, Pamela.

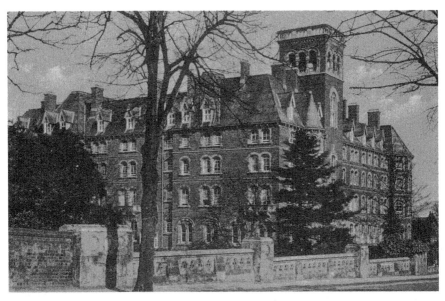

Malvern Girls' College, Worcestershire.

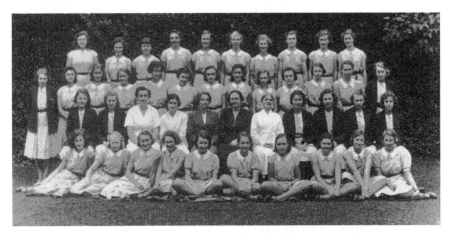

Lower IVth at Malvern. Frances is front row, far right.

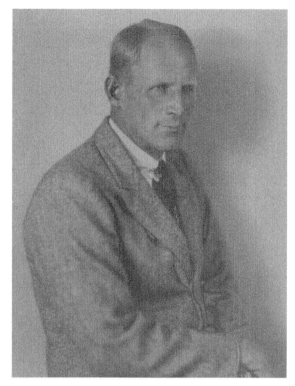

Claude Maguire Whitehead, Frances's father.

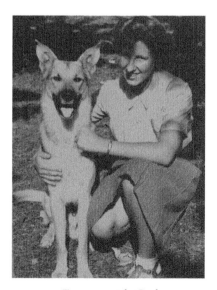

Frances with Carlo.

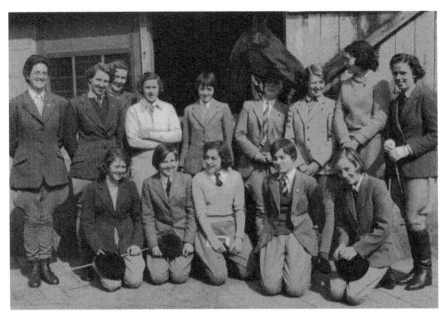

Girls' riding camp, c. 1955. Frances is second from the left.

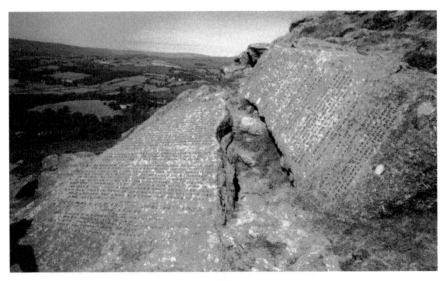

The Ten Commandments, a cherished landmark. Its 1500 characters were refurbished in 2017. Now in the hands of the National Park Authority.

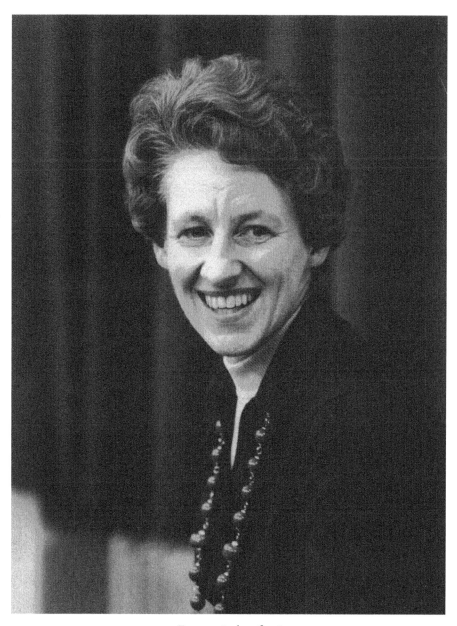

Frances in her forties.

PART IV

John Stott's Secretary (1956–2011)

CHAPTER SEVEN
New beginnings and new projects

A few days after Frances's meeting with John Stott, in which he had seemed unenthusiastic about her exploring Bible college, she was sitting at her desk in the BBC, typing a script for her boss. The telephone rang, with a personal call for her:

'Hello.'

'Hello, Frances. It's John Stott.'

Frances gasped with surprise at this unexpected call.

'Hello, Mr Stott.'

'Well, have you thought about it?'

'Thought about what?'

'About becoming my secretary.'

'Oh, I didn't think you were serious!'

So the Rector's alternative idea had not been fatuous after all. Her despondency at the end of the meeting had been quite misplaced. Frances agreed to think and pray about the matter, and to let the Rector know her decision. She had already sensed that her future did not lie at the BBC. Now, it seemed, it was unfolding in an unexpected way, at least for the next stage. No advertisement, job description, interview process or terms and conditions. Just a series of conversations in which John Stott had seen evidence of spiritual growth, a desire to serve, and clear ability in administration. The evangelical world was to turn on this kind of informality for a further thirty years.

At 9.00am on 9 April, 1956, Frances Whitehead, newly-appointed as the All Souls Church Secretary,[27] arrived at the Rectory at 12 Weymouth Street, about five minutes walk up Portland Place from her former office at the BBC. There was no overlap with her predecessor. In fact she was not allowed to meet her predecessor! One assumes that the previous appointment had not proved a success; Stott wanted a clean start with Frances.

The first surprise to greet Frances that day was that the Rector was not there. He was on a writing retreat at The Hookses, a house of which she had not heard.[28] John Collins,[29] the senior curate, saw Frances into her new job. She sat at a manual typewriter on the leather-covered kidney desk which had belonged to Sir Arnold Stott,[30] John Stott's father, which was placed in the corner of the large, south-facing first floor drawing room, furnished with two sofas and some comfortable armchairs. This somewhat quaint arrangement was different in every way from her office at the BBC.

Frances gradually met the Weymouth Street community. The Rectory was a six-storey Georgian house, far too big for an unmarried Rector, and soon after Stott had been appointed to the role, in 1950, he had approached the Church Council for their agreement that he offer accommodation to curates and three or four other single men who were church members. The house became known as the Wreckage (combining the words rectory and vicarage) and rather more irreverently as the Stottery. There was a housekeeper and a cook.

The housekeeper was Gwen Packer. She had lost her fiancé in the First World War, and never married. Packie, as she was known, took Frances aside early on, and in Frances's words, 'talked in no uncertain terms about how I was to behave.' Packie had seen a succession of secretaries come and go. Would Frances be another in the line, she wondered. Packie felt fiercely protective of the Rector, sensed the importance of the work which was piling up, and did not want to see another casualty. Frances, somewhat surprised at this unexpected feature of her job orientation, reassured Packie that her purpose was to support her boss in his ministry. Unbeknown to Packie, Frances had already given careful thought to the possibility of unhelpful emotional attachment; she had huge respect for the Rector, and was not naive. Indeed she had already begun to pray – and would continue to pray, that God would protect each of them from becoming a snare to the other. For the next fifty-five years Frances would work more closely with John Stott than anyone else, and those reassuring words to Packie were consistently borne out. We explore their relationship further in the next chapter.

A new office culture

As is always the case in a new role, there was much for Frances to learn. John Stott had his own systems, some quite detailed. He showed her his preferred way of putting stamps on envelopes, and the most efficient way of loading envelopes. Less easy for Frances to grasp was the evangelical world. She knew little of it, or of John Stott's growing engagement beyond All Souls. As the weeks went by, she began to build a wider picture through reading correspondence, and typing responses. This in itself was a demanding task as her boss could dictate between fifteen and twenty letters a day, some requiring her to research information, or insert enclosures.

As well as processing a huge correspondence, fielding phone calls, and handling the usual range of sundry tasks which make up office life, Frances also answered the door bell. In those days there was no entry phone for the front door, so every push on the bell required Frances to run downstairs. Her time at the desk was continually interrupted; it was all part of the job. The Rector's interviews with church members were generally scheduled for fifteen minutes. So she would run down the stairs, answer the door, and show people to a seat in the hallway outside his study, where they waited for the previous conversation to finish. In addition, there were other visitors on parish business, and homeless people, who would come for food. The hungry homeless would always receive help, either in the form of sandwiches, or a token for a meal in a café near Middlesex Hospital, in the parish, where the church had a special arrangement.

Now that John Stott had a secretary on whom he could rely, he began to take a day a week away from the Rectory. This gave time to plan and pray, and handle matters needing careful thought. These days provided a sense of distance, offering a measure of perspective not attainable in the rush of parish life. As Stott's name became well-known nationally, he was gradually receiving an array of invitations to write and to speak. He needed God's help in knowing what to accept, and knowing how best to take forward new strategic initiatives. To gain this time, he had to be sure the ongoing admin work of the parish and of his wider interests was in reliable hands. In Frances he had someone whose judgment he trusted.

There was a formal air about 12 Weymouth Street. Everyone called Stott 'Rector', while he would use people's Christian names. As time passed, a greater informality became discernible between Frances and the Rector. Gradually she handled more and more on his behalf, and became the interface between him and all those who contacted him. It was not long before he referred to her as 'Frances, the source of all knowledge' and then, until the end of his life, as 'Frances the Omnicompetent'.

John Stott's disciplined use of time became legendary. His pastoral interviews of fifteen minutes meant getting straight to the point. Hour-long conversations with leaders of churches or mission agencies would conclude after fifty-five minutes, with time to pray briefly, say goodbye, and collect papers together for the next meeting. This level of output requires a secretary who can brief well, work quickly, grasp issues, and anticipate needs. Mark Labberton, Study Assistant from 1980-81, described the basis from which John Stott worked. He had, said Mark, 'a drive for clarity, a confidence in rationality, an expectation of competence.'[31] It is not surprising that earlier secretaries had found it difficult to cope with the demands of the role. To satisfy that 'expectation of competence' demanded speed and intelligence. And, given the wider context of Frances's work for the first fourteen years until 1970 (that is, the week-by-week ministry of a West End church) it needed more; for it also required the patience, smile and sense of compassion expected then as now for the staff of any church office.

As letters arrived from All Souls missionaries around the world, Frances built up a greater feel for world mission. Stott responded punctiliously to all correspondence, using a dictaphone, and signing letters by hand. His responses were invariably thoughtful, detailed, and compassionate. Typing these deepened Frances's grasp of the issues faced in cross-cultural ministry, the challenges of raising families separated by continents when sending children away for education; the difficult decisions called for when parents become frail. Frances sent on news to the leader of the fortnightly church prayer meeting, and included newsworthy snippets in *All Souls*, the church magazine. For fourteen years she was responsible for the section 'Between Ourselves', which tracked all comings and goings.

One vital aspect of church life was the follow-up of new Christians. Everyone received an invitation to an 'at-home' in the Rectory; these gatherings were held monthly in the drawing room at 6pm, so people could come straight from the working day. Frances would ensure the room was set up and ready, her desk cleared in the corner. There would usually be twenty to thirty present, including the nursery class leaders, of which Frances herself was one.

Winnie, an elderly member of the congregation, would faithfully deliver rock buns for the 'at-home', in a tin which was tied up with a piece of string. The tin and the string would be returned to Winnie, and would appear again with another batch of rock buns, on the day of the next at-home. 'Winnie's buns' were a legend in their time, not always perhaps of the best consistency, but she herself was solidly consistent in her desire to help. Fortified by tea and Winnie's buns, this was a chance for new Christians to meet one another, and to meet leaders of the nursery class which they would be invited to join. John Stott or one of the curates would address the gathering briefly. John's talks became very familiar to Frances, and later to his Study Assistants: The new Christians were most likely to hear the 'ABC' talk: Admit, Believe, Confess; or the 'Know, Show, Grow' talk, illustrating how we need to know the truth of the Christian faith, live it out, and grow spiritually. His talks, written on 5 inch by 3 inch cards, were always concise and well-honed. Frances would file these notes, as she filed his sermons, in a manner which was easy to retrieve, so material could be recycled.

Frances as a nursery class leader

Almost sixty years later Shirley Done recalled Frances's commitment to her nursery class. Shirley first met Frances one Sunday evening in All Souls in February 1960, having arrived in London to train new recruits in the Midland Bank. She had ventured into the church with little Christian background. It was a guest service, and John Stott was preaching from Revelation 3. Shirley found herself listening hard. While convicted of her need to respond to Christ's offer to come into her life, Shirley didn't take up the invitation to talk with someone; after the service she was reflecting on her own, and about to leave when Frances came to sit beside her. Shirley recalls Frances's presence and bearing, and her welcoming spirit. Frances led Shirley to faith in Christ, and invited her to join a nursery class in the Rectory on Tuesday evenings when a group of women met to learn more about the faith they had committed themselves to.

Shirley joined the class having a sense of the gospel record from schooldays, but she was unfamiliar with the order of epistles. So when asked to turn to 1 Thessalonians, she did not know where to find it. Frances leaned over with a mnemonic to help her find it [referring to the first vowel in the name of each recipient church]: 'A E I O U, but turn the U into another E'. It took a moment to work it out, but lasted a lifetime, and Shirley could still hear Frances's voice when leafing through the epistles.

Frances invited Shirley to be a co-leader of the class the following year, and Shirley also became a commissioned worker. This 'hands-on' training which Frances herself had received as a young Christian, was invaluable for her future ministry. For Shirley that ministry would be as a mother and grandmother on the family front, and as a member of a small church in West Yorkshire, as an encourager.[32]

A Countess and a fake vicar

From early on, Frances showed remarkable versatility. Everyone in the Wreckage ate together around a large table in the basement dining room. When Packie retired in the mid-1960s, leaving only the cook to handle domestic arrangements, there was no-one to do the food shopping. This shopping can take significant time for a household of twelve people. Frances took on the role, adding it to her already-demanding task list. She soon established a pattern each week of filling up John Stott's car at a wholesaler's in St John's Wood. While returning the car to the garage behind the house after one such shopping trip, Frances was met by Countess Hella De Fries – a regular visitor at 12 Weymouth Street. No account of those years in the Rectory would be complete without a word picture of the Countess, Danish by birth, and a cousin of Karen Blixen.[33] The Countess, as she was always known, had professed faith in Christ through the ministry of All Souls, having got to know John Collins. She resolved to stay longer in London, and lived in a bedsit, while a frequent visitor to the Ritz and Savoy hotels. Her wide range of interests included car mechanics, and she was John Stott's self-appointed on-site mechanic, regularly seen in overalls, tinkering with his car. As Frances drove in, she met with the Countess's rage. For the Countess had, the previous day, loosened the engine bolts, unbeknown to Frances, and severe damage could have been done to the engine by driving it in this state. Whether the driver herself would have been in personal danger did not seem to feature in the Countess's ire.

While Frances did her best to guard the Rector from interruptions, at his request, he was never too busy to drop everything in an emergency. If news arrived of parishioners being taken into hospital, or of children becoming ill, the Rector would be there. He was very conscientious, with a real pastoral heart. Frances could sense how he would respond to matters, and knew when to interrupt him. For fifty years, Frances Whitehead would be John Stott's gatekeeper.

John Smith, a Wreckage resident in the 1960s, while working at North West London Polytechnic,[34] found the idea of Frances's impervious system of protecting the Rector just too tantalising. With assistance from the theologian David F Wells, a fellow resident at the time, who had become a Christian through Stott's mission to Cape Town University in 1959, he conspired to force a crack in it. John Smith recalls:

I guess scores of people would each day try to reach John Stott by dialling LAN 1867, but will not have accounted for the indomitable Frances.[35] Yes, she will have been amicable and tactful, but determined. If John did not wish to be, or could not be disturbed, then the caller could plead unceasingly, but Frances would remain resolute!

Personal callers at the Rectory front door would similarly not gain access to the Rector unless of course they had an appointment. No personal caller would get a foot across the threshold unless they had an appointment and Frances of course kept a duplicate of the Rector's diary.

This provided me with something of a challenge, as well as an opportunity for a little fun one winter's afternoon. I borrowed some props from other residents – a dog collar and black stock from Michael Wilcock, an old raincoat from Cook Kimball and a trilby from Seraphim Lopez, then, having donned them, I blacked out one of my front teeth with a Chinograph pencil, removed my spectacles and rang the doorbell. As planned, David Wells passed Frances's office to answer the door before she could get there, and to let me into the entrance hall. When Frances heard conversation below, she rushed down the stairs to investigate, only to be greeted by this unknown reverend gentleman who had come to see Mr Stott.

As I held out my hand and greeted Frances with my fictitious name, she did not recognize me and appeared very perturbed. It was a strange experience, having this momentarily different relationship with Frances. She insisted that there was no possibility of me seeing Mr Stott that day, nor any other, without making an appointment. I feigned perplexity, but could not retain my poise and within a few seconds surrendered. Her Majesty was not amused! She hurriedly ascended the stairs mildly annoyed and resentful of the disturbance from her work. Typical of Frances, she was immediately forgiving – and when I checked some years later, the prank was erased from her memory.[36]

New ideas and initiatives

From the late 1950s, Stott was coming up with new ideas and handing them over to others. Here we will see only a few of the initiatives taken and the part Frances played in their early establishing, to give a flavour of the far-reaching influence of her ministry, in support of John Stott's own. Some initiatives were local, others national and international. On the local front, within the All Souls congregation, a group was founded called the Philadelphia Fellowship for those exploring the possibility of Christian ministry with a mission agency, at home or overseas, or considering ordination. It was named after the 'open door' in Revelation 3:7 as its members were exploring which doors of service to open. The Philadelphia Fellowship met quarterly, with a speaker, and for several years was run by the curate, John Lefroy. Frances was responsible for its correspondence and record-keeping, and for sending invitations and reminders to its members.

On a national canvas, there was an annual gathering of church leaders who minister to students. By the end of the 1950s, John Stott had conducted missions in the universities of Oxford, Cambridge, and Durham, and had defended the cause of evangelical truth in the student world in a memorable exchange in the columns of *The Times*.[37] Now, working with Douglas Johnson (always known as DJ), General Secretary of the Inter-Varsity Fellowship, and Oliver Barclay,[38] a friend from student days, John drew together an annual gathering of Ministers in University Towns.[39] Here church leaders would listen to a 'state of the nation' address given by DJ, discuss major issues bearing on the student world, and identify church vacancies near university campuses, to encourage evangelicals to apply for them. Initiatives like this brought extra pressures for Frances, with the usual practical matters – correspondence with speakers, catering arrangements, and mailings to members.

A group of Anglican friends within the Inter-Varsity Fellowship formed a movement to work to foster greater evangelical influence within the Anglican Church. As with so many of Stott's initiatives, it grew. In 1960 it re-constituted itself as the broader (ie in breadth of membership, not in doctrine) Church of England Evangelical Council

(CEEC) which would become the founding member of the global Evangelical Fellowship in the Anglican Communion (EFAC).[40] Lists of committees and movements can make for stodgy reading. But their work was not stodgy. Men like John Stott, Oliver Barclay, DJ, and Alan Stibbs[41] did not deal in stodge. But much time was indeed spent in meetings. And wherever Stott was chair, or provided the secretariat, it added to the pile on Frances's desk.

The CEEC was to gain a strong foothold in England. The pastor-theologian J I Packer addressed a meeting in Cardiff from which it was hoped a Welsh counterpart would grow, but there was too much disparity among church leaders in Wales. Not wanting to broaden the evangelical footing of CEEC, it was instead resolved that individuals be admitted to the English CEEC as affiliate members until such time as a Welsh branch could be formed; a small group in Wales, perhaps eight or nine, began to meet at The Hookses, and in due course a Welsh branch was constituted. In a clear desire to influence thinking in the Church of England, a series of short books was published in the 1960s under a new CEEC imprint.

As each of these initiatives gained momentum, Stott would hand over the leadership, and Frances would be relieved of the admin. But the flow of correspondence would continue; and Frances would remain as the 'go-to' person for her deep background knowledge, and her ability to connect people on John's behalf.

'A life, not a job'

In 1963 John Stott broadcast a week of talks for the BBC Home Service *Thought for the Day*. He offered a copy of his booklet *Becoming a Christian*, a chapter taken from his 1958 book *Basic Christianity*, which was to become a two-million bestseller. The response to these talks was remarkable, and letters arrived by the sack load over the following few days, some six thousand in all. Frances worked to produce responses, and, where needed, to answer particular questions. These responses were then personally signed by John and mailed in batches, as fast as they could be processed, at the Post Office just around the corner from the Rectory in Great Portland Street. Frances handled many letters written in reply to this mailing, and where appropriate sent a further chapter from the book, also in booklet form, *Being a Christian*. Seven years into her role, the pace was relentless.

All the while, Frances was filling spare moments with the typing of John Stott's handwritten manuscripts. He wrote all his books by hand, and Frances prepared them as typescripts for the publishers. The first book Frances typed was *Basic Christianity*, destined to be translated into over fifty languages, formed from the substance of the addresses Stott had given in Cambridge University in 1952. Frances sent copies to her mother and to Sylvia. It seemed an appropriate gift for several reasons. It described the essence of her faith; and, she having typed the manuscript, it was in a real sense the work of her own hands. Further, it acted as a way of introducing her boss to them. Frances's mother was pleased to receive it; Sylvia less so.

In Frances's early years as John Stott's Secretary, Ann Bates and she moved to a rented flat in Devonshire Close, just a few minutes' walk from the Rectory. When the leasehold of the property was offered for sale some years later, Frances decided it would be good to invest in this way, and made the decision to purchase it.

Four pencil etchings by the eighteenth-century painter Thomas Gainsborough had come down into Frances's possession after her father died. They had been given as payment in kind to her great-grandfather Henry Whitehead for legal work done by his Chelsea firm. The client who paid in this way, a Mr Pierce from Cadogan Place, was a friend of the Gainsborough family, and had received the etchings as a gift. Frances took them to Sotheby's in New Bond Street to have them valued, and they were offered for auction. These etchings from a painter's pad in the mid-eighteenth century would enable her to purchase the flat, with a small loan from her mother.

Devonshire Close is a cobbled mews set off the street, with narrow houses built above garages, which originally formed a stable block. It is part of the Howard de Walden Estate, in common with almost the whole of Marylebone. Frances's flat was on the second floor, sharing an entrance with the first floor flat. The sitting room, with a bedroom on either side, overlooked the street at the front and a courtyard at the back. If Frances had her windows open on a warm summer evening, she would sometimes hear Jacqueline du Pré playing her cello, across the courtyard. A skylight window above the sitting room offered access to a roof garden. Henry Whitehead's informal way of settling accounts was to give his great-granddaughter a London home for more than fifty years.

In addition to what was already a diverse role, Frances, for twenty years, was also John Stott's driver, so he could use his travelling time for resting or thinking or working. She drove him to many meetings and conferences out of town until his Study Assistants took on this task. While at conferences, Frances would press her admin gifts into service in whatever way was needed. These could be pressured times, as all those know who have been near the nerve centre of events which run smoothly. There was often work to do late at night, with last-minute typing and copying.

Stott trusted Frances's judgment on many things, spiritual, social and practical. For example, she would occasionally buy presents on his behalf, if he could not find time for shopping himself. And as he did not have a great interest in which car he drove, he tended to follow her lead. So when he needed a new car, reluctant to give the time to researching the merits and demerits of different makes or models, he would depend on the research Frances had done in choosing hers, and then follow suit – a Vauxhall, Austin, Ford.

It was, as Frances reflected with a sense of satisfaction as she looked back in her eighties, 'a life, not a job'.

CHAPTER EIGHT
Changes at home enable wider reach: 70s & 80s

As the 1960s progressed, John Stott became widely recognised as an evangelical statesman. He was the leading proponent of a thoughtful, biblical evangelicalism which would withstand attacks from outside the church and from within it. His leadership would, in the line of his mentor Charles Simeon, maintain a three-pronged concern for expository preaching, world mission and social justice.

Why change was necessary

He could not, however, give proper attention to a parish church in the West End, as well as to the increasing number of invitations overseas, and to his writing. Radical change was needed, for his own role and for Frances's role, if he were to fulfil the ministry to which he sensed God's call.

This urbane Englishman had an unusual ability to cross cultures. His father had hoped he would be a diplomat, for which he exhibited all the natural gifts and abilities. While he pressed these gifts and abilities into service, it was not for his Queen or her government, but rather as an ambassador for Christ himself. In parallel Frances Whitehead's own role was changing and expanding, as she fielded more and more calls and correspondence from other countries.

John Stott was gaining a hearing for the truth of the biblical gospel in universities around the world. As university missioner, he would place himself under the guidance and authority of student leaders, and deliver a week-long series of talks, as he had done in Cambridge in 1952. In each place he would lay out a reasoned case for the Bible's authority, then, with the passion of the Apostle Paul in his heart, present the claims of Christ as God Incarnate, born to die on the cross to bring forgiveness for sin. Stott's presentation of biblical truth was reasoned and intellectually coherent.

As he planned the year ahead, he allocated blocks of time in his schedule with care. He did this before invitations arrived, to ensure he was in control of his diary: time for leading his staff team at All Souls; for travelling and speaking; for study and writing; for new initiatives. But increasingly the demands he sensed it right to fulfil grew beyond the time available.

While his international travel had initially been for student events, a further strand of ministry began in the 1960s. In October 1966 Stott was in Berlin to give the Bible Readings at the World Congress on Evangelism, convened by Billy Graham. The gathering traced its beginnings to discussions six years earlier in Montreux, where a small consultation was held at Billy Graham's initiative, to look at 'God's Strategy in Mission and Evangelism'. Frances typed Stott's paper on 'The strategy of Satan' looking at persecution, moral compromise and false teaching from Acts 4-6.

As Billy Graham and John Stott looked back to the 1910 World Mission Conference held in Edinburgh, it was clear that the World Council of Churches (WCC) had been one of its indirect fruits, yet the breadth of the WCC and its lack of doctrinal clarity led to little strategy for evangelization. Two years after the meetings in Berlin, in 1968, Stott was in Uppsala as an official Advisor at the World Council of Churches, invited to bring an evangelical voice. Again, it was a gathering for which he needed careful preparation as well as time for correspondence afterwards. That same year he had been in Mexico, to address a gathering of pastors. Each trip brought demands for Frances as for John. Preparations for the meetings and for absence bring inevitable challenges, and add pressure to the periods between trips. The curates, too, bore heavy loads.

A radical decision

As Stott thought and prayed about the way forward, he outlined a plan for an additional role, namely that of a vicar who would handle the parish ministry, and relieve him of this aspect of his work.[42] In his mind was a scenario where he and Frances could give their joint energies to his university missions in the UK and abroad, his writing, and whatever else issued from the Berlin meetings. He discussed the idea over breakfast one day with Dick Lucas, Rector of St Helen's, Bishopsgate, in the City of London, with whom he met regularly.

Dick Lucas saw sense in the plan and suggested Michael Baughen's name as the potential vicar. Michael Baughen was then the Vicar of Holy Trinity Platt in Manchester. Would the Baughen family explore a move to London? The leadership of All Souls is a Crown Appointment, on the recommendation of the Prime Minister's Appointments Secretary in Downing Street. So, Michael Baughen could not take over from Stott as Rector, unless he were appointed by the Crown, for which no guarantee could be given. The move from his growing work in Manchester, where he had just completed a major building project, would mean a big upheaval for the church there as well as for his family, and with no small element of risk. Like Dick Lucas, Frances too sensed a rightness in the plan; she more than anyone knew the extent of the pressures on John, and lent weight to persuading Michael Baughen to accept the invitation.

Over forty years later, in a book of tributes presented to Frances at All Souls on her official retirement in 2011, the Baughen family page read: 'That first morning [when John Stott had asked Michael Baughen to consider taking over] you drove Michael across London urging him all the way to say "Yes"!' In a letter a few months later, following John Stott's death, Michael, recalling those days of irresolution, wrote: '. . . indeed would we have said "yes" without your eager persuasion?!'

As soon as the Baughen family agreed to the move, plans were put in place for changes, and an announcement made in both churches. All Souls would, from 1970, have a Rector and a Vicar. When Michael Baughen, his wife Myrtle and their three children moved south, the Rectory once more reverted to being a family home.

Frances relocated to the ground floor, into what had been the cook's bedroom. So she exchanged her leather-covered kidney desk in the south-facing drawing room, which ran across the width of the building, for an L-shaped desk in a compact, newly-created office, with a filing cabinet and photocopier, a large shelved cupboard, a chest of drawers from the Stott family home; and for visitors, a Parker Knoll chair, which had been used in one of the bedrooms in the Wreckage. Her view had gone, as the windows looked out onto a brick wall. While she had enjoyed the natural light of the drawing room, there was little time for admiring views.

A small one-roomed flat above the garage at the back of the house, facing north up a narrow cobbled street, Bridford Mews, was extended upwards to provide John Stott with a two-roomed flat. It had a bedroom and shower room, with a spiral staircase leading up to a sitting-room-cum-study and a galley kitchen. This flat could be accessed through the Rectory, as well as through its own door at the new address of 13 Bridford Mews.

The culture of Weymouth Street changed overnight, as Michael introduced himself to his new staff team by his Christian name. The Wreckage residents dispersed, and a new ministry, dedicated to the global church, modest in its staffing and facilities, became established. All Souls was now under Michael Baughen's leadership in all but name. He interviewed for a church administrator to take over the work Frances was handling for All Souls, and Frances's job title was changed to 'John Stott's Secretary'.

Being freed up from the leadership of All Souls, yet remaining anchored in it, was the spiritual genius of Stott's ministry. He could not have delayed longer. The Berlin gathering led to the historic 1974 International Congress on World Evangelization in Lausanne, Switzerland. Here Stott was chief architect of *The Lausanne Covenant*, which issued from it, and which came to be regarded as one of the most significant documents in modern church history.[43] On it the Lausanne Movement was founded.[44] John Stott and the Lausanne Movement would share a symbiotic relationship over more than twenty years. *The Lausanne Covenant* reflected his major concerns for the global church, and the exposition and commentary he wrote on it gained remarkable traction.

In 1975 Michael Baughen was appointed by the Crown as Rector of All Souls Church, from which time Stott became known as Rector

Emeritus. It was an irregular arrangement for a Rector Emeritus to continue to live in and work from an adjoining flat behind the Rectory, and for his secretary to retain an office in what was essentially the Baughens' home. While indeed unusual, it reflected the unusual, indeed *sui generis,* nature of John Stott's ministry. Frances continued in the same office on the ground floor of the Rectory for over forty years, as 12 Weymouth Street became home next in 1983 to Richard and Elizabeth Bewes, and from 2005 to Hugh and Clare Palmer.

From the time John Stott had handed over to Michael Baughen as vicar in 1970, a new Trust had been set up. The Church Commissioners provided one salary only for the Rector of All Souls, which would now be used for Michael Baughen's appointment; so Stott's own salary, Frances's salary, and the running costs of their new ministry, which would include from its early days the help of a Study Assistant, would need to be raised independently. For this purpose The Langham Trust was formed, called after the street address of All Souls Church in Langham Place.

Substantial sums were coming in as royalties for Stott's books (which were in due course published in some 60 languages, and sold in millions) but that money had been irrevocably assigned to fund Christian literature in the majority world. New money would have to be raised. From the outset, Frances administered this Trust, which began with gifts from a few friends.

The work of the Langham Trust drew a solid mass of letters daily for Frances's attention and sorting; each needed a response: invitations to John Stott to speak or to write; confirmation of arrangements for meetings; requests for Stott's advice on personal matters or his views with regard to theological and social trends. Frances pelted through a huge volume of work.

Grace Jackson, Frances's flatmate in the early-mid 1970s, recalled how Frances 'would arrive in her office in Weymouth Street at 9.00am promptly and usually didn't get back to the flat until well into the evening. In addition to her work with John Stott, she led a weekly group for new Christians which met in the evening in Weymouth Street, and a fortnightly fellowship group which met in Devonshire

Close, and which alternated with the church prayer meeting; and she was a member of the PCC.' It was a pace of life which never let up.

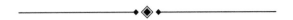

Mark Labberton arrived in September 1980 as John Stott's third Study Assistant. One of the things which surprised Mark, who had just completed his Masters degree at Fuller seminary in Pasadena, Southern California, was the quality of the office furnishing. There was a modesty about it, as there was about the whole Langham Trust operation. But was there too much frugality? Frances was sitting on an ordinary upright dining room chair, rather than on an office chair, with a swivel seat and castors. Chairs with castors had been standard issue for all desk workers for a considerable time.

> 'I would see Frances laboring with great effort to pull open very long, heavy, file drawers. With her characteristic swiftness, Frances would unselfconsciously lean all the way down and use her full weight to heave them open – repeatedly throughout the day.
>
> 'I asked her if she wanted to have castors on her desk chair at least. She memorably looked down quizzically at the legs and said, "Don't I have them?" We laughed and laughed. This led to some office changes that were minor, but revolutionary to her.'

When Frances had first arrived, and sat at Sir Arnold's desk in the corner of the drawing room, she had simply accepted that church furniture was likely to be less up-to-date than that in the BBC offices. So she had used the upright chair for twenty-five years, oblivious to its inconvenience, despite the number of times she ran down to answer the door or moved across to the filing cabinet. Placing this in its wider context, Mark Labberton added:

> 'John and Frances did as a twosome on a shoestring what for many others would have taken a staff on a large budget. They revelled in each other's efficiency and thrift. They did all this with a sense of being good stewards of limited resources, and seeking to make a real difference in the lives of others. It was part of both of their commitments to simple lifestyles.'

Frances typed with a sheet of carbon paper beneath each page, in a manner hard to imagine by anyone born after the seventies. The carbon paper lay face-down beneath the top sheet, with a lighter-weight page under it, and often with a repeat layer of the sandwich, to produce two carbon copies. The 'cc' ('carbon copy') click on an email address list bears no relation to the practice after which it is named. The distance travelled by each typewriter key when pressed down was considerable, and keys needed to be pressed hard, so the metal characters which sprang up to hit the inked typewriter ribbon would have sufficient force to leave a clear impression on the paper behind it; more, the depression had to be hard enough to go through to the carbon copy, or the two carbon copies. This constant pressure of typing, together with the continual shunting of the typewriter carriage at the end of every line, made the process a much more strenuous activity than it is now.

The manual typewriter would give way to the electronic typewriter in offices and in homes in the 1960s and 70s. But it would be 1980 before such upgrading of equipment in Weymouth Street, with encouragement from Mark Labberton. When Mark later returned to the UK for his doctoral studies in Cambridge, he introduced Frances to a Mac computer; and she would remain a Mac user from then on.

A remarkable partnership

Few could have had an accurate mental image of the way John and Frances operated. The scope, reach, and effectiveness of his growing global ministry was based solely on this team of two, with a Study Assistant and occasional admin assistance for Frances. It was an operation which would bemuse, indeed be-fox, any management consultants.

With evident care for the woman who had invested her life in his ministry, John Stott would always ring Frances on Christmas Day and on Easter Day, just to greet her, as well as on her birthday. In addition, when travelling overseas he would call when he arrived. As well as marking Christmas and birthdays (often with a hardback biography, for example of Chuck Colson, Solzhenitsyn . . .), there were occasional impulsive gifts, like an embroidered Indian silk shirt from Karachi airport as they changed planes on the way to Pattaya; a Welsh tweed coat and skirt in deep heather purple from the woollen mill in St David's; a gilet for walks at The Hookses . . . 'He was always very generous,' recalled Frances.

In the pressured office days, the working partnership was inevitably close, as Frances needed to know John Stott's mind on matters. All requests for Stott's time would come through Frances; a system which never changed. For his ministry to be effective, this was necessary. Some found Frances over-protective; that was bound to happen. Her unique access to her boss was envied by several women who would have liked more of his attention. 'It is hard to imagine, said Mark Labberton, 'that this relationship did not cause some perturbations, being two single people working platonically side by side throughout so much of their lives.'[45]

Clearly John's and Frances's ability to work together so closely for so long was a mark of grace. Two single people of similar age working long hours, under pressure, in pursuit of the same goal, would, for most mission agencies or churches now be avoided. It is a tribute to both of them that for twenty years, before the Study Assistants arrived, they succeeded in working so closely as a team of two. They both had a high level of inner discipline, partly innate and perhaps partly the product of their upbringing and education. While unspoken to one another, they resolutely did not allow for romantic hopes to take root; embarrassment and awkwardness would have undermined a remarkable working friendship.

It was a unique partnership, and one for which the English language perhaps has no word. In an age which underplays the dignity of serving, it is hard to understand that aspect alone of Frances's make-up, a woman so able in her own right. Her role was textured, layered, diverse. Their partnership has been described as a kind of 'marriage without the marriage'.

'During my years as Study Assistant,' recounts John Yates,[46] 'a number of friends asked me if John and Frances had ever considered marriage to each other. No doubt this was a question also asked more widely.' He continues:

> It made me pause to consider the nature of their long and fruitful partnership. Their relationship was unique, not least in the nature of their deep, mutual affection. They both had a very clear sense of vocation: John was to serve Christ's church through a ministry of writing, preaching and encouraging younger leaders; Frances was to serve Christ's church through serving John – making him more efficient and effective. They were passionately committed to their intertwined vocations and both saw the great grace of God in the gift of each other. While intertwined at the deepest level, however, there never seemed to be an unhealthy co-dependence or a longing for something more in their relationship. There was a sense of joy in standing alongside each other and serving together.

Mark Labberton observed of their working together: 'It was a relationship of mutual honor and love, respect and affection, playfulness and partnership, independence and interdependence. John was able to do what he did because Frances was able to do what *she* did. They were both fast, exacting, and determined.'

Tom Cooper, in 2011, describing himself as 'second Study Assistant in the apostolic succession' wrote in Frances's retirement book: 'You are unique from all others. You understood John, and the calling God gave him in the church. You . . . helped him successfully and faithfully to fulfil his calling (or dare I say both your callings).' The legacy sketched in the Appendix bears witness to Cooper's assessment; it was a double calling, a joint calling; and one which needed driven and focused attention from each of them.

Some people found Frances's efficient telephone manner a little intimidating, not least when combined with her somewhat dominant personality (the shyness and reserve of younger years having diminished with time) and the timbre of her voice, marking her distinctly upper-middle class background. Telephone conversations were short, and straight to the point. A Scot serving in the IFES[47]

International Service Centre in Oxford recalled how she always sat up straight in her chair when she called Frances, and an IFES colleague from the northwest of England said 'I would put on my best southern accent when I called Frances.' There was no doubt that Frances Whitehead commanded respect. But while speedy in all her office conversations to redeem the time, she had much personal warmth, which she retained throughout her life.

For Frances to know how to help the callers best – in terms of giving them access to John (or in the days pre-1970, to a curate), she had to know what they needed. For those who wanted to see Stott himself, rather than a curate, she would require information about the nature of their request. On the strength of this, he could then allocate the appropriate amount of time – fifteen minutes, thirty minutes, a full hour – and brief himself for the meeting. While some felt Frances intrusive, even obstructive, there was good reason for her manner of handling each request.

As with all jobs, stress at work is sometimes created by a set of particular circumstances; sometimes just by the sheer volume of work; sometimes by tight deadlines. For Frances there was often a confluence of these factors. So much of John Stott's interface with the evangelical world was from the platform, or by way of the printed page, both bringing a time-critical frame to the delivery. Some people – inside the evangelical church as well as outside – would parse his statements carefully, to identify where they considered him wrong. If backlash was inevitable for standing for the truth, or indeed for standing for greater breadth within scripture's boundaries, he was prepared to receive it. But he did not want to stir controversy through an ill-chosen phrase. Nuance mattered. Register mattered. Context mattered. And sometimes if the completion of a weighed response was so close to the wire, because of the volume of other work to be done, pressure could be intense.

Lausanne Movement gathers in Thailand

In June 1980 John Stott and Frances Whitehead flew to Bangkok, for the Congress on World Evangelization in Pattaya, Thailand (COWE, mischievously referred to by some as COWEpat), run by the Lausanne Movement. It was to be held in the city's Cliff Palace Hotel. As with all Lausanne meetings, the onsite staff had largely been seconded by their organizations, and arrived from several countries, most not knowing many others. A coach was waiting in Bangkok to meet flights and take people to Pattaya, and Frances got onto it. John Stott, however, did not take the coach, as he was to join other committee members in visiting the nearby refugee camp which had become home to thousands of Cambodians during the scourge of the Khmer Rouge years.

A month earlier, on 12 May 1980, Frances had typed a memo from John Stott to Leighton Ford, which formed a draft of a public statement, to be distributed to participants and made available to the press. It anticipated questions about the venue – both its comfort and its geographical location. How could a movement committed to a simple lifestyle justify a Congress on world evangelization taking place in a luxury hotel, just a stone's throw from Kampuchean (Cambodian) refugee camps? As Stott explained, there was no single 'right' place to hold such a gathering. Airfares would almost always cost more than accommodation; and the timing, with 'the appalling Kampuchean disaster' had placed the Lausanne Committee in a serious dilemma. But moving elsewhere would not take away the problem of the camps. Thai church leaders had urged that the booking remain, and the Committee resolved that they should make best use of the camps' proximity, by visiting the camps before the Consultation. This would enable them to share news with participants, and they would plan a day of fasting to express solidarity with the refugee organizations, and to support them financially. The memo concluded:

> '. . . we shall assemble there in a chastened mood, both penitent for our share in a world system which causes such tragedies, and resolved to play some part in redressing the injustice and relieving the suffering.'

On the evening of the fast day, two OMF missionaries, David Pickard and Don Cormack, delivered powerful, passionate accounts of the plight of refugees from Cambodia and Laos and Vietnam.[48] The

Lausanne Movement was especially sensitised to Cambodia's plight. Taing Chhirc, a Cambodian major in Lon Nol's army, had been at the 1974 Lausanne Congress, and then at the Keswick Convention in the UK, pleading for prayer for his country as he could foresee the terrible times ahead. In response to his plea, OMF had sent a small team to Cambodia, all single people, as there was no guarantee of their safety. Major Chhirc was martyred the following year, within a few days of the fall of Phnom Penh to the Khmer Rouge.[49] The mood of the Congress was rightly as the memo had captured.

Frances had typed much Lausanne Movement correspondence since the planning of the first 1974 gathering in Lausanne, Switzerland, but had not herself been to a Lausanne gathering until this one. She had on several occasions sent copies of draft memoranda to a range of people asking for comment, as this one to Leighton Ford, and counted in the responses. Consultation in this way was one of Stott's strengths, partly to refine his own work, and partly to gain a broader ownership of a completed statement. Such consultation always brings much gain, but it is labour-intensive. Frances saw its worth, and shared John's commitment to this way of working, even though it multiplied her work at significant pressure points, before and following major events. Based on scripture's teaching that there is wisdom in the counsel of many, consultation was a principle which stretched to all John Stott's endeavours, Lausanne and its working groups being only one example.

Frances had been looking forward to the Pattaya meeting with a sense of expectation. She would see Christian leaders from a range of countries with whom she had been in touch, and some she had met in Weymouth Street. It would, she knew, be a stretching and enriching two weeks. Regular newsletters had been mailed to all two thousand five hundred participants from November 1979, with updates on the planning. A major part of the Congress would be spent in 'mini-consultations' on specialist issues, and Stott was to co-ordinate this aspect of the programme, meeting throughout with the consultation chairs and recorders. Working in specialist groups is always more efficient and productive than simply having a programme of plenary meetings. But it also creates more work for the programme committee, and for the administrative staff. To service the groups, many papers had to be photocopied and distributed each day.

Naturally, one of the practical aspects of preparation for such a congress is the ordering of paper. Sufficient stocks had been ordered, and had arrived at the airport. As is customary in a tropical climate, the Pattaya June rainfall comes with little warning, and the pallet of paper for the Congress was inadvertently left on the runway and got completely drenched. This necessitated some quick thinking for the Thai hosts in sourcing replacement stock. Where events are seen to run as smoothly as a swan glides, it is almost always the result of much paddling beneath the surface.

An angel in East Anglia

Seven years after the Pattaya event, in 1987, back in the UK, the third National Evangelical Anglican Congress, NEAC3, took place. These NEAC gatherings were the shop window of the CEEC. Here Frances worked into the night with Toby Howarth, John Stott's then Study Assistant. The planning of this particular event had included some difficult discussions. The first two NEACs, held on the university campuses of Keele (1967) and Nottingham (1977), had both attracted significant attention in the UK broadsheets as well as in the Christian press. Both congresses had wrestled with critical issues in a nation where, at an ideological level, the Christian faith was becoming increasingly-more marginalised by secularism and pluralism; yet where evangelicals were gaining in numerical strength and influence in the established church.

Plans for the third NEAC were to take on a different feel. John Stott wanted to see a major statement issue from this Congress, and for there to be a serious publishing programme from it, to extend the benefit of the event. The planning group was not convinced of the need for this. They chose for its location the Caister Haven Holiday Park on the Norfolk coast, rather than a university campus, and resolved that the 'C' of NEAC should, this time round, stand for 'Celebration' rather than for 'Congress'. The programme design reflected this with less emphasis on working groups and a greater emphasis on communal praise. The planning group invited Stott to give the morning Bible studies, relayed into chalets, and to chair a 'listening group' throughout the long weekend. He was also invited to give the final address on the Sunday evening in the Big Top marquee.[50]

Some closing addresses can, to an extent, be shaped in advance, with amendments made onsite, during the event. But less so for a closing address which had to reflect the findings of a listening group. In the pressure of the last full day, as the listening group reported back, the final amendments were worked into the address. Frances duly revised the script, but it was not ready to be printed out until after John Stott had left for the evening meeting. So the new plan was for Frances to ensure it got to the Big Top to reach him while he was sitting on the stage, before he stood up to speak. Words had been weighed; phrases crafted; an argument had been built from a biblical principle with careful illustration, all fitting the timing allotted. The minute-by-minute plan for the evening had been made available to all taking part, so it was clear exactly when Stott would need to have the speech in his hands. Unknown to everyone in the Big Top, including John Stott himself, there was a moment of crisis.

Frances was printing off the speech in her chalet as planned, ready to grab it and ensure it reached John. But somehow in her rush she managed to shut herself out of the chalet, without the speech. John Stott would soon be on his feet, and he kept glancing over to the wings, expecting his speech to appear. It was not his style to speak off the cuff on such occasions. The finely-crafted address, entitled *What is the Spirit saying?* comprised five sections broken into subsections; it could not be re-constructed in the air. And given the concern that at least some outcome of the 'celebration' be published, the delivery of this address was crucial.

Frances prayed for help. The weighed words; the crafting; the alliterative argument; the sensitively-expressed yet uncompromising conclusions – there they lay on the printer. Frances looked around for someone to come to her aid. There would be a doorkey at the site Reception, but the Holiday Park sprawled, and Reception was some distance away; she knew she would not be able to run over and back quickly enough. Along the rows of chalets there was no-one to be seen as everyone was in the marquee. What should she do? This was in the days before mobile phones were common. Suddenly a man appeared from nowhere, listened to Frances's story, and hared off in the direction of the office to collect the spare key.

Shortly afterwards John Stott stood up, walked over to the podium, and placed his script in front of him.[51] He was soon taking his characteristic pose with his right hand on his script, his left hand in his pocket. Frances never saw the man again who had helped her. It was, as she recalled twenty-five years later, her closest encounter with an angel sent by the Lord.

CHAPTER NINE
The growth of a global ministry: 1956 onwards

John Stott had first received an invitation from InterVarsity/USA and Inter-Varsity Canada in 1953, to speak at university missions in North America. He felt unable to accept, but hoped that a time would come when this would change. He responded with regret, to say that he could not leave London for such a trip at this stage.

Frances's appointment brought the change. Seven months into her role, October 1956, saw particular pressure. The North Americans had renewed their invitation, and John Stott was to leave for North America, to lead evangelistic missions in nine universities.

The university Christian Unions across the Atlantic were younger than those in the UK, and this would be their first such mission weeks. As Stott did not imagine further invitations coming quickly, he had asked the churchwardens if he might consider an extended trip, given the distance involved, and they had agreed. He allocated four months, which gave Intervarsity, his North American hosts, good scope, but necessitated a great deal of planning in London, for John himself, for Frances, and not least for the curates.

Frances left London early on 4 November, 1956, to drive to Guildford, to collect John's mother, Lady Stott, and his sister Joy, to take them to Southampton docks to say goodbye. He would spend his first week at Toronto University, then move to the University of Western Ontario[52] and Michigan State; it was a tight, solid program. After Christmas he would lead missions in Manitoba, British Columbia (Vancouver) and McGill, then at Harvard, Yale and the University of Illinois. Not surprisingly, Christmas 1956 was to be spent in Montreat, California, at the home of Billy and Ruth Graham and their family.

Frances had been much involved in all the correspondence about this trip, with InterVarsity staff, with student leaders in the universities, and with Tony Tyndale, a former member of All Souls, who, with his wife, Penelope, would accompany John throughout the trip. It was to prove a pivotal speaking tour in the universities for the thirty-five-year-old Rector. Stott's gifts as an evangelist in the university arena had been used well in the UK. From this point onwards he would receive invitations from all continents. Having grown in his faith in his own student days in Cambridge, the student world became one of his chief priorities.[53]

Four months was a long absence for a parish minister. During this time Frances worked with John Collins, the senior curate and with the bursar John Dugan. She handled all the correspondence which came in, seeking advice when needed; and – as in all of John's subsequent absences – was able to give blocks of time to typing his books. As John Stott's global travel increased through the 1960s, so did the range of questions Frances received from people he had met around the world. He was a pastor, a leader and a friend to hundreds with whom he spoke personally. Frances would endeavour to answer questions and engage with problems on his behalf.

A teenager in Mexico

So, for example, in 1967 a letter had come from a thirteen year-old boy in Mexico, Saúl Cruz.

He had just read *Cristianismo Básico* (*Basic Christianity*) right through, three times, and had found faith in Christ. But he still had questions, and he believed only the writer of this book would understand them and take the time to engage with them: questions about poverty, and about Christians he had met personally who had died for their faith. He decided to write a letter to the author, and to send it to the book's publisher, in Argentina, for it to be forwarded.

Many weeks passed, and young Saúl had almost given up hope of a response, when an envelope appeared at home, wrinkled and marked, bearing a British stamp. The letter was from Frances Whitehead. She had received his letter and called in help to translate it, and to formulate a response in basic Spanish. As he read, Saúl learned to his disappointment that El Tío Juan ('Uncle John', by which Stott was becoming known to students around the world), did not speak Spanish. However, he would be in Mexico the following year to address a pastors' conference, and Frances was sure that he would be happy to respond to Saúl's questions. The following year seemed a long time to wait, and the conference was being held in Mexico City, three-hundred miles northeast of where he lived. But Saúl's hope was not easily abandoned.

Now aged fourteen, Saúl set off, against his father's wishes, and hitch-hiked from his home in Oaxaca City to downtown Mexico City, and the Methodist Church where the meetings were to be held. The sessions themselves were translated into Spanish, but the teenager, tired and hungry, soon drifted off to sleep. As Saúl had no English at the time, there was little opportunity for more than short conversations through an interpreter that evening, and again the next day before he began the long journey back to Oaxaca. While conversation had not been deep, Saúl had been touched by the Englishman's kind face, and his authenticity, for these transcend language. It was some years before Saúl and Uncle John met again, by which time Saúl was a university student, and had learned English. But his reading *Cristianismo Básico*, followed later by other Stott titles including *Grandes oportunidades y retos para el cristianismo hoy* (*Issues Facing Christians Today*), would shape the direction of his future, as we shall see.

Scheduling travels

Schedules for overseas trips were always tight, and careful crafting of an itinerary was needed for optimal use of time. Stott's Autumn Newsletter of 1972 illustrates the care taken in the planning of a US trip, in which he was to be based at Trinity Evangelical Divinity School in Deerfield, Illinois. He writes, 'I am to give one course of lectures and seminars in biblical preaching, and two or three other courses in books of the New Testament.' Then, tellingly, 'These lectures are being concentrated midweek on Tuesdays, Wednesdays and Thursdays (including a Thursday evening course for visitors from outside the college), then I shall be free at weekends to fulfil other engagements.'

The weekends would be spent at ten American Colleges, delivering a lecture based on his UK Presidential Address to the Inter-Varsity Fellowship, entitled 'Your Mind Matters'. This took him to nearby Wheaton College, also in Chicagoland, to New England (Gordon College), to Washington State (Seattle Pacific University) and down to Southern California (Westmont College). On five weekends he would address student leadership conferences of the US and Canadian Inter-Varsity movements. In addition, he reserved one whole weekend for the emerging American branch of EFAC. Needless to say, birdwatching would also fill some cracks in his schedule. Correspondence. Planning. All the swapping around that is always needed when one piece of a jigsaw doesn't quite fit. Then finally booking flights. Frances Whitehead took such scheduling in her stride, alongside the ongoing work of Stott's wider ministries.

The pressure did not let up as Newsletters show. Twenty years later (March 1994), John Stott's Newsletter was written on his return from a US tour. He had, at the beginning of the year, spent two weeks in Kenya and Tanzania. Now he and Frances were preparing for his upcoming travel in Asia, in May: 'beginning in Bangalore and Madras, continuing in Singapore and Sabah, and ending in Malaysia. In each place I have been invited to address pastors and / or theological students. And during this journey and my two January weeks in East Africa, I expect to renew fellowship with a dozen of our Langham scholars, which will be a special joy.'

Travels for the rest of 1994, he said, would be limited to Europe: Slovakia (church-based), Warsaw (student evangelism conference), Holland (Lausanne Forum of Bible Agencies) and Romania (consultation on theological education and leadership development in post-Communist Europe). Each name listed in the Newsletter was shorthand for often quite detailed arrangements for the meetings, and for all the follow-through correspondence afterwards. Meeting after meeting after meeting would all be managed from Frances's desk.

When the departure day arrived for each overseas trip, Frances would drive John to Heathrow airport, and she would meet him on his return. Richard Bewes, who followed Michael Baughen as Rector of All Souls in 1988, recalled how, from his study window in Weymouth Street, he would see Frances 'bundle John and his luggage into her small blue Vauxhall.' There was a rather delightful and stark incongruity about Stott's travels, which few saw. For as Richard Bewes continues: 'In some places he would be fêted, feasted, interviewed, filmed and garlanded. Then he would fly back to Heathrow, where Frances would be waiting for him with the little blue car.'

John's return from travels always brought an onslaught of correspondence. He followed up diligently on conversations, sent thank-you notes and not infrequently a book as a gift, and he sought to steer towards further study those he met with the most able minds. Particularly from the mid-late 1970s, as John Stott was known as Uncle John around the world, so Frances Whitehead became known and loved as 'Auntie Frances'.

Stott's overseas travels were to extend deep down in each continent. For as the years passed, each region became a group of clusters in both his and Frances's thinking: IFES national movements where Uncle John would address staff, students or regional events; members of EFAC; seminaries and pastors benefiting from books provided through the Evangelical Literature Trust / Langham Partnership; old friends who were keen birdwatchers, and so on. There was indeed, as John Stott would frame it in his tribute to Frances on her sixty-fifth birthday, an 'evangelical underworld'.

Twenty-five years

In 1981, Frances Whitehead marked twenty-five years as John Stott's Secretary. Stott was given a sabbatical break that year to mark his 60th birthday, and Frances would also have sabbatical leave. The London Institute for Contemporary Christianity (LICC) would open the following year, and its planning was very much to the fore. The anniversary of the actual day Frances began work as All Souls Church Secretary was a date John always marked, often with a letter of appreciation. He was at The Hookses that April, and posted a letter to Frances. It was written on the morning of the anniversary, on personal writing paper, with his characteristic light hold on a black biro:

9 April 1981

My dear Frances

I ran out of superlatives years ago in my verbal attempts to express my gratitude to you. So, having exhausted my limited vocabulary, I labour under considerable difficulties! All I can say is that I thank God constantly for you, for that providential day 25 years ago when you crossed the road [from the BBC to All Souls] and for your truly astonishing versatility, conscientious efficiency, workload capacity, persistence and personal devotion. People sometimes ask me if I realise how lucky I am. I think I do. And now I pray that you yourself will have a marvellous 'long leave', and will return reinvigorated for the LICC stage of our partnership, and will find great satisfaction in it.

The enclosed is meant to help you persuade yourself to be a little extravagant sometimes on the Continent. You can regard it as coming partly from Joy,[54] since it is her money which enables me to do it easily. But it's really a token of my tremendous gratitude.

Yours as ever

John

Frances and Rose McIlrath planned an itinerary that summer through France, Switzerland and Italy. It was a holiday with many memories. They arrived in Cannes at the time of the Film Festival, drove at a leisurely pace through the Loire Valley, ran into a fierce rain storm at one stage which took a windscreen wiper off the car, and had to barricade the door of their room one night when a drunk was sure it was his room.

One sweet memory was of a five-year-old girl with whom Frances fell into conversation. 'Pouvez-vous parler plus doucement?' the little girl asked. It was a surprising request from one so small, and amused

Frances, who did her best to comply. It took Frances back to her early conversations with Lady Stott, who asked her to temper her voice by speaking more slowly.

On one Sunday, while based in Vilars in Switzerland, they decided to join the congregation from Francis Schaeffer's L'Abri, a large English-speaking gathering in the Alps. They hadn't bought anything for lunch that day, as they were sure someone would invite them out. When they discovered the theme of the service was practising hospitality, and the sermon based on Hebrews 13:2, they had no doubt this would happen. However, no-one spoke to them, and they left laughing that evidently they would never be confused with angels in disguise! The following week they worshipped as a congregation of two in the Marne Valley. As Rose recorded in her journal: 'We awoke to a cloudless sky, had breakfast and were soon on our way to our self-appointed kirk; a kirk with cows and kites, in other words a stubble field.'

From Vilars they went to visit the great sights in Florence, Pisa – and of course Assisi – the city of Francis Maguire's patronal saint, whose name had passed down the family; and then Rome. Here they walked along the Appian Way, and visited the catacombs. Rose wrote in her journal:

> We descended to the Mamertine prison, where Paul and Peter were most likely held, in its lower cell. The only entrance for light, food and people was by a single hole in the ceiling, which was low (just clearing Frances's curls), and the floor sloped to a central drain. A large iron door led to a culvert, and there was a hovering stench. On one wall there was a stout iron pillar which had manacles, to which presumably the prisoner was attached.
>
> It was a very awesome spot; one could scarcely conceive of anyone writing such disciplined letters: words of comfort, exhortation to patience and to endurance, and to an ordered and controlled life, as we have in 2 Tim. Paul was surely called to suffer great things for his Name's sake. I am so grateful to have visited this place.

The London Institute

The diverse strands of John Stott's global ministry were to be drawn together in 1982, in his founding of the London Institute for Contemporary Christianity (LICC). He was sixty-one and Frances, fifty-seven. This was to bring a poetic sense of completion interwoven with new beginnings. St Peter's Church in Vere Street, where Frances had first heard John preach, would have its pews removed, a seminar room and offices built around the nave; and a library built upstairs in the gallery. Once the conversion work was finished and an academic faculty appointed – a mixture of salaried staff appointments and volunteers – this Institute would serve the global church in two ways. It would host training courses, of which we learn more in the final chapter, and, informally, it would expand networks. Uncle John had met many young leaders around the world through his work with university Christian Unions. If they could come to London, the Africans, Asians, Europeans could meet one another and learn from one another. Stott was the founding Director of the Institute, and he taught at least one course for each intake of students in the annual thirteen week 'Christian in the Modern World' (CMW) programme, which took place each autumn.

Frances had been heavily involved in all the planning for the London Institute since the idea first formed in John's mind. She enjoyed getting to know the students with whom she had corresponded. John would invite students to his flat in small groups, and Frances would join him. Each cohort brought familiar names from different contexts: emerging leaders of IFES movements; promising young graduates who would enter academia, or medicine, or the business world; pastors on sabbatical leave. It was through such encounters that Frances Whitehead's knowledge of the evangelical world grew to be so extensive. As the years progressed, more names would be added to the database to receive John's twice-yearly newsletter.

It was now more than ten years since the arrival of Michael Baughen, and John Stott's books were being published in over fifty languages, strengthening the church in some of its toughest contexts. Through his writing, his teaching and preaching, and his personal investment in the lives of many individuals, Stott's networks were unparalleled. As Mark Greene summed up for the Memorial Service in St Paul's Cathedral, 'He wrote for millions, preached to thousands, but, Jesus-like, he invested in individuals.' Looking at a cross-section of the evangelical church on any continent would illustrate this, and show the role Frances played. Take the Americas.

In the Institute's fifth year, the autumn of 1987, Frances would finally meet the thirteen year-old Mexican boy with whom she had corresponded years earlier. Saúl Cruz, now a clinical psychologist married to Pilar,[55] had met Uncle John again as a student; and their paths crossed once more in September 1987 at the Lausanne Younger Leaders' Gathering in Singapore. Saúl was on the staff of World Vision, and John Stott invited them both to participate in the CMW course at LICC.

It was a late invitation and would take some juggling, but they were keen to accept. They would need to arrive a day or two into the course, and were unsure where they could stay. As they were getting ready to fly, Saúl telephoned the Weymouth Street office from Mexico. They knew John was away, and wanted to find out when he would be back. To their relief and surprise, they found themselves talking with Frances Whitehead, who immediately recognized their names. Shortly afterwards, when she greeted Saúl and Pilar Cruz in London, it began a friendship which would extend to the next generation, as we see. Following their time at the London Institute, Saúl and Pilar founded a ministry, Armonia (translated Harmony or Shalom), to minister among the poorest of the poor, in Jalalpa, a huge rubbish dump on the west side of Mexico City, where shelters built of milk cartons kept out the rain.

The Latin culture is warm and welcoming; it was not easy for Latin American Christians to arrive in the UK and meet with British reserve. Ziel Machado from Brazil recalled his first encounter with Frances on the morning he began his course at the London Institute. 'Frances approached me with open arms, addressed me by name, and said she had been praying for me, and for my time at the Institute to be a blessing. It was the best welcome I have ever received.'

Ziel had first met John Stott in Brazil in 1989. Aged, seventy-seven, Ziel was the young General Secretary of the IFES movement in that large country. As Stott talked with young gifted leaders he no doubt recalled his own early days as a twenty-nine year-old Rector in a West End parish. He was a shrewd judge of character and of a person's potential, and he invited Ziel to come to the London Institute for applied theological study, and undertook to make a scholarship available. They corresponded for two years, and Frances wrote to Ziel several times over that period. Ziel, a modest man, had resolved not to say much in the course, but to listen and learn. Then, as he explains, 'One day Uncle John urged me, "Please Ziel, change your mind. I would love you to share more about the situation of the church in your country. We all could learn from that."' LICC was a place of community, of learning from one another, and of sharing together in the gifts Christ has given to his church around the world. The Latin Americans brought much from which everyone, and not least the Northern Europeans, could learn.

The Stott – Whitehead Library

In May 2005 Frances opened a letter from a lawyer in El Salvador, Mardoqueo Carranza. He too had studied at the London Institute. Mardoqueo had recently founded a training centre linked with his church, the Centro Biblico Christiano in San Salvador. The centre was planning to open a new library, much helped by gifts from Langham Partnership. Mardoqueo's letter held a completely unexpected request. It was for Frances Whitehead's agreement that the library be named after her, in recognition of her fifty years of service to John Stott. Frances was deeply touched at the proposal, but felt unsure how to respond. She needed time to think and pray, and to consult with John on the matter.

On 28 June 2005, she wrote:

> It has taken me some time to know how to respond to your very kind suggestion that your new library be named after me. I was totally amazed and found it hard to believe that you were really

being serious! But I naturally feel greatly honoured that you and the board members of the Centro Biblico Christiano Church should want to celebrate my 50 years of working with Uncle John in this way.

I have now had time to think and pray about your proposal, and to discuss it with Uncle John, and I wonder if you would be happy to accept a compromise proposal, that the library should be named after John Stott as well as me? Humanly-speaking, I owe my entire Christian faith and ongoing discipleship to Uncle John's ministry – it was under his preaching in the early 1950s that I came to believe in Jesus Christ, and if it had not been for his teaching and example, there would have been no 50 years at all!

So with Uncle John's agreement, I would like to suggest that you name your new library as follows:

> The John Stott – Frances Whitehead Library
> In celebration of his 60 years' global ministry
> And her 50 years in support of him

If the title is too long, then please just call it 'The Stott – Whitehead library'.

I look forward to hearing from you again, and meanwhile thank you so much once more for your proposal – I pray the Library will be greatly used in the future in the ways which you describe.

A year later, Frances was thrilled to receive photographs of the opening of the library. It had taken place in May 2006 with Ruth Padilla Deborst as the speaker.[56]

News of honours

John Stott's ministry was increasingly recognized by the secular world and in April 2005 America's *TIME* magazine listed him as one of the 100 most influential people in the world, giving Frances a huge measure of satisfaction. In 2006, his name featured in the Queen's New Year Honours list. He would receive a CBE, that is, be recognized as a Commander of the Order of the British Empire.

Frances had opened the envelope from Buckingham Palace, with the news, a few weeks earlier, but it was made clear that no-one should be told before 31 December 2005, when the lists would appear in full in the UK press. It was a wonderful and fitting honour for a Chaplain to the Queen, and Extra Chaplain after that period of service drew to completion. But would it be misunderstood by John's friends and partners in the gospel around the world? How would friends in the former colonies respond? Would his acceptance of the Honour come across as imperialistic? Stott had always been sensitive to the way his Britishness could be perceived: an urbane Englishman from a privileged background ministering in very different contexts in the Majority World. He recalled how his being a Chaplain to the Queen had itself proved difficult in Kenya on a university mission in the early 1960s, as the country waited for independence.

John, Frances and Tyler Wigg-Stevenson, John's Study Assistant, talked about it, and worded a careful email which would be sent around the world as soon as the news was public. It explained the honours system and clarified that this did *not* mean that John would become 'Sir John'. Most importantly, it added that while he was grateful for the honour, and particularly for the citation which read 'for services to Christian Scholarship and the Christian World', he was somewhat embarrassed by the continuing reference to the 'British Empire' which long ago ceased to exist! Frances Whitehead would accompany him to Buckingham Palace to receive the honour, together with his two nieces, Caroline Bowerman and Sarah Meinertzhagen.

CHAPTER TEN
The happy triumvirate: 1978-2007

From the outset, the staffing for the new Langham Trust with its global reach was modest, and its office space was also modest.

Frances's small office was on the ground floor of the Rectory. Stott operated from a desk in his study-cum-sitting-room, in front of a north-facing bow window on the second floor, in the newly-constructed flat above the garage at the back of the house. His small bedroom below doubled as a corridor for visitors, who would have to walk through it; and as an office for the Study Assistant, who had a desk – rescued from a skip – in one corner.

An engraving of Charles Simeon, striding through Cambridge with his umbrella under his arm, hung on the staircase. John Stott, while still a Cambridge undergraduate, had been introduced to the writings of Simeon by Douglas Johnson. Simeon was known for his fashionable dress sense, and his umbrella was one of the first in England. He was vicar of Holy Trinity Church in the centre of Cambridge, for over fifty years. John had been into this church hundreds of times, as it hosted the weekly evangelistic address for the CICCU,[57] and more than once he had stood in its East end, reflecting on the memorial plaques to Simeon, and to his curate Henry Martyn.

Charles Simeon became John Stott's mentor as an expositor, and in recognition of that John stated in his Will that he wanted the words of Simeon's memorial plaque to be used in due course on his own headstone.[58] Simeon referred to his team of two curates, Henry Martyn and Thomas Thomason as 'this happy triumvirate'. It was the term, gender notwithstanding, that John began to use for himself, Frances and the rolling list of Study Assistants.

Miss Doom takes reality checks

Each Monday morning, the happy triumvirate would meet for breakfast in John Stott's flat. As well as catching up, and praying for the week ahead, this would be the opportunity for John to share with his team any new ideas or new projects in his mind. Frances could recollect no occasion when anything was pushed through as decided without prior discussion. John knew everything would depend on his team and would never move ahead without first making sure he had consensus in a happy, and not coerced triumvirate: happy with the direction and happy with the tasks. Frances brought a keen eye for detail, and an instinctive sense of how much work would be needed behind the scenes to achieve each stage. She could sometimes voice caution, but she would never impede. The whole triumvirate – its effectiveness and indeed its happiness – was oiled on willing spirits; it could not have functioned otherwise. This was the context in which many a project began. Once the core team was on board, John would discuss ideas with a few others.

John Stott sometimes called Frances 'Miss Doom' for her habit of sounding a note of realism into the breakfast discussions. She could see in her mind's eye the new lists to be constructed, the emails and the chasers, the separate financial accounts, the new mailings needed. Of the three, Frances undoubtedly had the best information about other time-commitments, and was best-placed to calibrate how a new plan could be integrated, and made to work. Many an evangelical venture goes no further than the Minutes of a meeting and the good intentions of those whose initials appear in the Action column. This is inevitable to an extent in understaffed mission agencies. The happy triumvirate however, while lean to the bone in staffing, would remain in clear control of what they took on. While calling Frances 'Miss Doom', Stott at heart recognised the value of her reality checks. Matthew Smith (Study Assistant 2002-2005) recalled how Uncle John used to joke that his Study Assistant was sometimes right, he was mostly right, and Frances was always right.

In January 2000, John presented Frances with a limerick he had written for her, illustrated by his then Study Assistant, Corey Widmer. It was rather dryly entitled 'Conversion'.

Conversion

The ever-hilarious Frances
Expresses her joy in her Dances.
Tho' once called 'Miss Doom'
(for she used to spread Gloom)
Every hope she now finds, she enhances!

To mould an efficient team from three gifted, high-energy people, needs clarity on roles and good communication. Monday breakfasts were an anchor each week, and this was supplemented by much other interchange.

Frances's roles, as we have seen, were not always easy to define. In addition to handling John Stott's correspondence, fielding his calls and keeping his diary, she would also be a listening ear for the Study Assistants if they needed counsel, and if required, an advocate for them, as she knew John trusted her judgement.

Study Assistants' memories

One of the early Study Assistants, looking back nearly thirty years, recalled the way Frances 'combined diligence and availability in a way few have mastered'. He continues: 'She never gave the impression of being too busy to help. The only exception is one occasion I recall to my horror. As a single, insensitive twenty-five-year-old who should have known better, I noticed that a button on my new Harris Tweed jacket was coming loose so I asked if Frances would sew it on. (I half think this may have been a second offense - having been emboldened by earlier help. I have repressed the details.) I do vividly recall that she asked if the request was "fair". It was a rhetorical question and I was smart enough to supply the answer quickly.'

Greg Downes also recalls Frances's straight talking. Greg served as a locum Study Assistant before training for ordination at Wycliffe

Hall, Oxford. His ordination selection report had said he needed a 'spiritual director', and John Stott took on this role. He recalls how Frances took him aside, when he was aged twenty-two, and 'told me how blessed I was, given that John Stott declined to do that for most. I did feel very blessed.'

Later, having begun his training at Wycliffe Hall, Greg dropped into Weymouth Street for a visit. He had begun to put on weight ('the notorious Wycliffe stone') and again Frances took him aside. 'I should watch your weight if I were you,' she cautioned. 'John doesn't like to see fat clergy – he thinks it's a bad witness.'

'I wasn't in the least bit offended, but charmed by Frances's maternal and direct concern,' said Greg.

While the Study Assistants helped Stott with his research, and acted as Aides de Camp when he was travelling, their roles in Weymouth Street were as varied as Frances's roles. They would help him entertain small groups, in his flat; dive into archive libraries to track down quotes for his writing; and shop for him in Oxford Street if he needed new clothes to complete his modest wardrobe, for he had no interest in clothes shopping.

Their first encounters with Frances Whitehead tended to leave lasting impressions. John Yates III recalled his first experience of Frances, in 1996:

> On my very first day in the office at 12 Weymouth Street I was given a new name. There I was, just 21 years old, enormously jetlagged from my flight the previous day and thoroughly overwhelmed by the sheer energy of London. It was 9.30am and I had reported for duty before the desk of the singular Frances Whitehead.
>
> 'Now John,' she said in such a way that intimated slight disapproval. 'It is going to be altogether too confusing round here with two Johns in the office! I wonder, do you have any other names?' She spoke so quickly and with such authority that I was torn between my need to process what she had said, and the clear expectation of an immediate reply.
>
> 'Well', I stammered, 'when I was in college I had a nickname. A few of my close friends called me JY.'
>
> 'Right then,' she replied, 'JY it is!'

From that day forward I had a new name. During four wonderful years in London I was JY to everyone I met. Many folks never learned my proper name – Frances simply would not have it! And now, whenever I hear myself referred to as JY, I grin, inwardly remembering that delightful moment in which I was re-christened by her ladyship herself, Frances Whitehead!

Then capturing a fuller picture of 'her ladyship', he added:

How 12 Weymouth Street and The Hookses rang with Frances's joyful laughter! She could intimidate the socks off any pushy American in an effort to protect Uncle John, but when the happy triumvirate was alone in the office, or with close friends down at Hookses, Frances's ready, full-throated, head-tilting laugh was always just a moment away. I once heard a Presbyterian pastor, Earl Palmer, say 'the higher your Christology, the better your sense of humour.' Frances, in company with Uncle John, proved the truth of this statement.

In 2005, new Study Assistant Tyler Wigg Stevenson and his wife Natalie were expected to arrive around 8pm, having flown in from Los Angeles and hired a car at Heathrow. A flight delay meant they did not arrive until midnight. Frances would show them to their accommodation. Aged eighty, she was as alert as ever. 'Hello, you made it!' Her voice was to them 'an audible distillation of Britain'. Natalie, Essex-born, and having emigrated to Canada as a child, nudged Tyler and whispered: 'She sounds more like the Queen than the Queen does!'

Tyler writes:

After a warm, whirlwind welcome in her flat, Frances whisked us up and out and off to see our new digs in Cleveland Street, which is a seven-minute walk, perhaps more in the dead of night, when the weight of the preceding day slows the pace of mere mortals.

But we were there in five minutes, perhaps four – and that first walk was the perfect introduction to the year to come, in which not a day went by that I didn't need to stretch myself to keep up with the extraordinary Miss Frances Whitehead, nearly six decades my senior, and a force of (graced) nature on earth. My year at Weymouth Street was not a year with John Stott, but with John-Stott-and-Frances-Whitehead, as inextricable as they will forever be in the photo of them at the Buckingham Palace CBE ceremony, which sits now on my desk, Frances behatted and beaming.

Pressing time into service

Time mattered. John Stott used time as efficiently as he was able. He planned his year; planned his weeks; planned his days. So while he needed Frances and the Study Assistant to work to protect his time, it was to press it into service. He had no sense of self-importance. Indeed when Frances worked from the Drawing Room, he would frequently empty her rubbish bin, to save her carrying it down to the basement. This was a small symbolic act of his wider desire to serve.[59]

Protecting John Stott's time was not straightforward. As to be expected, there were those who found Frances over-protective, and did not understand why John was not accessible. But when John said he could not take any calls, she understood why. His articles, as indeed his books, were written in longhand. For there to be a lucid flow of thought, with structured arguments and clarity of expression; and for them to read, in the words of many a reviewer, as 'vintage Stott', with alliteration, and with carefully-chosen illustration, the crafting of each paragraph would count. This demands deep concentration, especially without a keyboard, which allows the continual progression of edits, now second-nature to most writers.

John Stott's output determined the pace for Frances Whitehead, and it was relentless. Frances once described her work to Toby Howarth (Study Assistant 1986-88), as being akin to driving down a narrow London street in a Mini, with a fire engine, lights flashing and siren wailing, speeding behind her. Toby said in that case, he felt as if he were on a bicycle, in front of both of them! Close friends of Frances could see on occasion that the pressure was almost intolerable.[60]

Celebrating birthdays

But days were not humourless, in Weymouth Street or The Hookses. Far from it! There was a culture of celebration, marking anniversaries and birthdays. John Stott had always marked birthdays, from the days of the Wreckage, when he would take the cook or the housekeeper out to the cinema to celebrate. The triumvirate settled into a pattern of celebrating Frances's and John's birthdays together, starting with dinner and then a show. The Study Assistant of the time would research what was on – *The Mousetrap, Xerxes, Les Miserables* – and bring a proposal to Monday breakfast. Tradition was broken after The London Eye opened, and they instead surveyed London from one of its pods.[61] JY recalls:

> It was the norm to eat dinner at a Chinese restaurant near Piccadilly (a meal accompanied by sweet German wine) and then go to the movies. Uncle John always paid for everyone. If there were a new James Bond film showing, that always won out over the others. During my tenure we saw *Tomorrow Never Dies* and *The World is Not Enough*. My most vivid birthday movie memory comes from watching *Titanic* while seated between John and Frances. In the film there is a scene with prolonged female nudity. During this seemingly endless scene Uncle John's absent-minded knee-tapping became rather more pronounced and rapid – the only sign of his discomfort. Frances remained absolutely still – not even breathing – until long after the uncomfortable moment had passed. I sank deeply into my seat hoping never to have to emerge.

Frances Whitehead's sixty-fifth birthday fell on Tuesday, 27 March, 1990. John, as so often before, took the initiative to ensure the occasion was properly marked, and invited fifty of her friends to a lunch party. In the UK, women were, in 1990, still tending to retire at the age of sixty. However, there was no discussion of retirement for Frances.

John Stott gave the toast as follows:

> Dear friends of Frances, your presence today – an almost 100% attendance of those invited who are in this country – is itself an

eloquent expression of the affection we feel for Frances and the high esteem in which we hold her.

Little did I imagine, after a watchnight service in All Souls in the mid 1950s, at which Frances committed herself to Christ, how much I would come to owe her. She has thrown herself without reserve into supporting the ministries in which I have been involved.

I think of her extraordinary capacity for work. For example she absorbed the office work for both the Evangelical Literature Trust and the Langham Trust scholarship programme, which now is handled by two separate administrators.

Then there is her speed. I know nobody who can type faster than she, and nobody who speaks faster on the telephone! Callers sometimes have to ask her to stop, start again and speak more slowly. Yet her speed does not impair her efficiency. She has high standards. In fact she's a perfectionist.

Next, she's a wizard with figures. It is not widely known that she handled all the covenants relating to the All Souls restructuring appeal. She has also been responsible for the accounts and budgets of the Langham Trust scholarship fund and other funds.

I don't need to tell you that she is highly intelligent and full of common sense. She also has the maddening habit in debate of nearly always being right!

She took just one day to master her Apple MacIntosh Plus. Since then her harassed computer has not been able to keep up with her. It not infrequently flashes on its screen what I understand is called a 'bomb icon', a kind of desperate appeal to the operator to slow down.

Frances also uses her hands in other ways. She is a skilled needlewoman, a knowledgeable gardener and a versatile cook.

In addition she is a gifted pastor and teacher. She loves people. She led a nursery class (as beginners groups used to be called) for many years, and has been a Fellowship Group leader for many more. I have met people in several countries who look back with gratitude to the teaching and care which Frances gave them.

Just three weeks ago in Sydney, Australia, the wife of a lecturer at Moore Theological College told me that she had been an appreciative member of Frances's nursery class.

It has been the same with our Langham Trust scholars. She has never been content merely to send them their monthly cheque. She also prays for them, and develops with them such a personal relationship that it is natural for them to call her 'Auntie Frances'.

Above all, I am thankful for her commitment to Christ, her spirit of loyal service, her invariable cheerfulness and her sense of fun.

Of course, she could easily have moved on to a top, lucrative, executive position in the City. But she has believed it right to stay in church work on church pay, and we admire her for it.

Her name is well known all over the world. Because of her unrivalled familiarity with the evangelical 'underworld', people telephone her for information about all manner of things. And burdened Christian leaders sometimes confide in me: 'What I need is a Frances Whitehead'. To which I reply, 'You can't. There's only one. And she's not available!'

In conclusion, neither Christian theology nor personal experience permits me to call Frances perfect! In some situations she can be pessimistic, so that I call her 'Miss Doom'. At other times she is guilty of hyperbole, so that I remonstrate with her 'Don't exaggerate, Frances!' But these are trifling peccadilloes. They do not inhibit me from applying to her the only word in the whole range of English vocabulary which seems to me to do her justice – and that word is 'Omnicompetent'.

So, ladies and gentlemen, I give you this toast: 'Frances the Omnicompetent, with much love and admiration.'[62]

A song had been composed for the occasion by Toby Howarth, then in Butembo, Zaire. He recorded it with Graham and Wendy Toulmin,[63] who had taught him in Sunday School at All Souls, when a boy. The tune was 'Guide me, O Thou Great Jehovah'. Toby and Wendy sang, with Graham on the trumpet. They posted the tape recording to Frances.

The Omnicompetent Frances

Let us sing of Frances Whitehead
Loved by many round the world
Sixty-five good years God's given
What a story could be told!
Auntie Frances, Auntie Frances
Omnicompetent is she!
More than just a secretary.

Frances first showed her credentials
When she ran the BBC
Now she runs another corporation
Balanced Biblical Christianity.
Auntie Frances, Auntie Frances
Omnicompetent is she!
Famed (and feared) for her efficiency.

If you walk into her office
Typing furiously you will note
That her powerful Macintosh computer
With her speed it just can't cope.
Auntie Frances, Auntie Frances
Omnicompetent is she!
Master of technology.

When she's in the Langham Trust mode
Pounds and dollars balance there
Then some lonely troubled stranger
Interrupts with their despair.
Auntie Frances, Auntie Frances
Omnicompetent is she!
Always having time to care.

So this wandering ex-Study Ass
Sounds his tribute from Zaire
Those two years were very special
You were wise and full of prayer.

> Auntie Frances, Auntie Frances
> Finally I'd like to say
> Thanks and love on your birthday.

The song was evidently appreciated, so much so that it was sung in All Souls the following Sunday, with the congregation joining in the chorus. As Mark Labberton, an earlier Study Assistant, described her, 'Frances was as remarkable in her own way as John Stott was in his.' For all who collaborated with John Stott – in the UK and around the world – Frances Whitehead was an institution.

Aboard Sea Cloud

In June 1992, Frances was invited by David Spence, an old friend and long-time supporter of John Stott's ministries, based in North Carolina,[64] to join a party of seventy, mainly US donors, for a trip aboard the tall ship *Sea Cloud*, the world's largest sailing yacht. The two-week voyage would take the party around the Aegean, exploring New Testament sites in Greece and Turkey. John Stott acted as the ship chaplain, and each evening he provided a commentary on what is known of the sites from the Book of Acts, Revelation, and the Pauline epistles.

Frances was accompanied by her friend Vivienne Curry[65] with whom she shared a cabin. They flew to Athens, where the tour began, joining those who had flown from the US. First the party walked to the Parthenon and the Aereopagus, then visited the Peloponnese cities of Corinth and Mycenae. From here they looped back to join *Sea Cloud* at the ancient port of Piraeus.

The Aegean cruise gave Frances and Vivienne new insights into the biblical narrative as they traced Paul's steps: Troas where Paul first met Luke; Pergamum, which for all its wealth and culture, was 'where Satan has his throne';[66] and on to Izmir, Smyrna, Sardis, Philadelphia, and Patmos, where John had received his Revelation for the churches. The tour party then took to buses to visit Miletus and Ephesus; and concluded with a day in Istanbul. It was a profound and invigorating experience.

On the last evening, light-hearted entertainment included the presentation with mock seriousness of spoof certificates, humorous trophies which summed up the characteristics of the travellers. Each was officially stamped, and bore the signatures of David Spence as High Admiral of Maritime Awards, Captain Shannon, and John Stott as Chaplain. To loud applause, Frances received the award of 'Grand Bazaar Bartering Queen'; and she and John shared the 'John James Audubon Award' for the keenest birdwatchers on board.

Taking stock of new needs

The happy triumvirate pace did not ease. And when John Stott began to suffer mini-strokes in the late 1990s, it was clear that some changes would be needed, if he were to remain fruitful and effective.

In 2002, Frances Whitehead and Corey Widmer jointly signed a memo on behalf of Stott's Advisory Group of Elders, to be sent to all who would be hosting him. He was now 81 years of age, and his peripheral vision was permanently impaired. He wanted to continue travelling for as long as he was able, so it was felt that hosts would need to have certain standards set out. All were modest requests. But importantly, there should always be an alternative plan, in case the visit needed to be cancelled at short notice.

The guidelines asked that no meetings be scheduled before 8.00am; that he be afforded an hour's rest on a bed after lunch; that no more than two major engagements be scheduled in a day – public lectures, media events etc; that he be allowed to retire to his room by 9.30pm; that there be one or two days off per week. To work to ensure this, they added: 'Please send us in advance a detailed and complete schedule of the proposed programme for John Stott's visit. Once a schedule has been agreed upon we ask that nothing be added to it without consultation.'

Frances and Corey asked that there not be constant travel, with two nights in any one location; that accommodation be simple – in a personal home rather than an hotel where possible; that urban centres be preferred in the Majority World, for access to health care should there be urgent need.

With impaired vision, John Stott would now need a four-foot lectern, with good light; and while he enjoyed greeting people after his talk, a limited time for that would be preferable. He wanted to be able to field questions, and these should be submitted in writing as it was no longer easy to field extemporary questions from the floor; and as he lived in a two-roomed flat, he had no room for gifts. A bird-watching excursion would, however, always be appreciated.

A few days before Christmas in 2003, both Frances and Matthew Smith, the then Study Assistant, received a call from John late in the evening. He had had 'a little difficulty' as he said to Frances, and 'a slight problem' as he explained to Matthew. This understatement was a small stroke. He was due to fly six days later to the Urbana Missions Convention in the US, to address 18,000 students. This would of course have to be cancelled immediately; and his medical Advisor, John Wyatt, urged that there be no travel for the following year. The Triumvirate's Team Talk notes in January 2004 record from Frances: 'I for one am thankful that after about fifty years [John] is at last going to be able to have a year free from overseas travel, and get down to all those other tasks which have constantly had to be put aside.' No-one was more aware of these than she.

One of the tasks too often pushed to the back of the desk was to compile *Through the Bible Through the Year*. The plan was for a daily devotional study book which worked through the seasons of the church year and the great themes of the Bible. Based around the church calendar, it could appeal to a churchmanship wider than evangelicals, and bring exposition, reflections, and pastoral application to readers who may not often encounter this kind of engagement with scripture. It was finally completed in 2005. It would be published the following year, dedicated to Frances, in celebration of her fiftieth anniversary as John Stott's Secretary.

CHAPTER ELEVEN
Life at The Hookses

The Hookses, a derelict farmhouse near Dale, in Pembrokeshire, on the West Wales coast, was to become a second home, and a second office, to Frances Whitehead. From early on in her role as John Stott's Secretary, she would drive to West Wales for around two weeks at a time, two or three times a year. John Stott had purchased the farmhouse towards the end of 1954, about eighteen months before Frances arrived in Weymouth Street.[67] He travelled there five or six times a year himself, leaving his senior curate in charge. Frances's roles at The Hookses would confound any dictionary definition of 'secretary'.

Access to The Hookses was not easy: up a narrow lane, through a gate leading onto the runway of a disused World War 2 airfield, then turn left and follow the runway for some six hundred yards, and then left again. Here was a farmhouse and a few outbuildings, built on a gradient bordered on one side by the airfield, on the other by the coastal path, and with commanding views across West Dale Bay. In Frances's early visits there, the house still had no mains drainage, relying only on a septic tank. Neither was there mains electricity, so oil lamps and candles were used for lighting, and a Calor gas stove for cooking.

Stott had first discovered The Hookses while on holiday with his friend and curate John Collins in 1952. It was remote, yet near a village, and the birdlife around it was rich; five miles offshore lay the bird sanctuaries and colonies of Skomer and Skokholm. By December 1954, John Stott was the owner, purchasing it with the advance royalties from his first book *Men with a Message*. Over the next several years, with the help from friends and family, and student working parties, The Hookses was painted, repaired, renovated and gradually extended.

It was always Stott's intention that The Hookses be made available to Christian groups for fellowship and study. Even though it did not have mains electricity until 1997,[68] Frances was taking bookings from the 1960s. These were for small house parties, often students from All Souls, or more geographically-diverse gatherings like the Writers' and Painters' workshop from the UCCF Christian Unions.

Transferring the office to Dale

The nearest shopping centres, Milford Haven or Haverfordwest, were both twelve miles away, so a car was essential. For as long as there was a night train running from Paddington, this was John Stott's preferred transport, so he did not waste work-time in travel. The Countess would drive him to catch the train at midnight. Frances, with Packie or others, would have left by car the day before, to take whatever was needed for the office, and to buy food. Frances would then meet John off the night train at Milford Haven. When the night train was discontinued, the pattern changed, with John, Frances and Packie leaving by car at 5am, for the long drive through the Cotswolds then stopping for breakfast at the The Swan Hotel in Ross-on-Wye, before descending into the valleys, past Abergavenny, Merthyr Tydfil, Neath, then Carmarthen, and joining the A40. Things changed dramatically with the opening of the M4 – first as far as the Welsh side of the Severn in 1971, and then through South Wales in 1993. Frances preferred to drive, as she felt John drove too fast. While history does not record the speeds, it can be inferred that Frances Whitehead was herself no slow driver. However her first speeding fine did not materialize until 2014, earned close to home, and to her frank disbelief. Hearing of it, a former Study Assistant remarked that he himself could bear witness to its being at least twenty years late in coming.

For decades, Frances's heavy old manual typewriter always travelled with her; there was no duplicate machine at The Hookses – another mark of office frugality. After Packie retired, Frances would take a friend with her, often Muriel Green, who worked with the Managing Director of Readers Digest, and later for Tearfund. On one occasion, Muriel Green and Rose McIlrath were both there, and had gone for a walk along the cliffs. When they returned there was no sign of Frances, or of John, and the car had gone. Frances had been typing the script for what became *Guard the Gospel*[69] and had carried her typewriter outside, to type on the terrace. As she carried it back into the house, she tripped, bashing her toe on the step, threw the typewriter in front of her and went down after it. In some considerable pain, and fearing she had broken a toe, Frances asked John if he would drive her to the hospital in Haverfordwest. In characteristic fashion he immediately picked up his Bible and book manuscript, along with the car keys, and they set off.

The doctor assured Frances the bone was not broken, and strapped it up. The pain continued, but John, from a medical family, kept reassuring her that she had to believe what the doctor said. Jocularly, as they arrived back at The Hookses, he called out to Rose, 'We need a vet!'

The following morning at breakfast, there was evidently still a problem. The local vicar's wife, a physiotherapist, was called. She unstrapped Frances's foot, and without ado pulled the toe, which gave an audible crack. The doctor was correct; there was no breakage. But he had strapped the toe in a dislocated position and trapped a nerve in so doing. John seemed bemused at this evident slip-up from the medical profession.

The pain disappeared, but Frances's typewriter did not recover. The fall had thrown the carriage out of kilter. Muriel, Rose and Frances scoured Haverfordwest for anyone who could mend a typewriter. Eventually the three friends managed to find a way to get it working again, by weighting the carriage at one end with a brick. This Heath Robinson solution held well for several weeks. The story was to be recorded in the final paragraph of the Preface of *Guard the Gospel*, published in April 1973:

> I express my warm gratitude to my secretary, Frances Whitehead, for her efficient and tireless labours during the past seventeen years, not least in the typing of innumerable manuscripts. She is not likely to forget this one, since it was the indirect cause of an accident which involved her in the pain of a dislocated toe!

> J.R.W. STOTT

John Stott would give an inscribed copy of each book to Frances on publication. This book's inscription, following an expression of gratitude and some jocularity over the toe incident, ended with the words, 'and with expectation of the years still to come.' Whether a lifetime calling had been verbalised at any stage earlier may not now be known, but the message here was clear.

Improvements over the decades

Throughout the 1950s, Stott would work at a desk in the main house at The Hookses, but in 1960, a member of All Souls, Charles Fairweather – who was a building contractor – constructed a study bedroom for him, by creating The Hermitage, a triangular building between two of the out-houses, and with a largely glass wall on its southern side, overlooking the bay. Here John Stott could store a library for whatever work he was engaged on at the time, and keep his copy of one of his favourite books, Saki's short stories, conveniently on his right. He would pick this up on many occasions to take with him to supper, when the working day would often finish, to read to his guests after the meal. On his desk lay his binoculars, for what Paul Weston, a member of the All Souls staff in the 1980s, referred to as 'an ornithological emergency'. In 1990, the Hermitage was extended to create a separate bedroom in a small flat, which would include an office for Frances. The lighting and heating here, as in the main house, were powered by calor gas until The Hookses was joined to the national grid, so electricity could be installed.

Joy Stott, John's sister, loved The Hookses and had been one of its earliest visitors to help paint, always accompanied by her unruly beagle, Fanny. When Joy died unexpectedly in 1979, John used his share of her estate to build a first floor extension to the house, with two further bedrooms, and a shower room; the larger bedroom was called Joy's Room, and the smaller Fanny's Room. Over the years, the out-houses were gradually converted into sleeping quarters as gifts were received; and a special appeal was made in honour of John Stott's eightieth birthday.

Frances generally slept in the Loft over the barn, which is now called Meg's Loft. Meg Allen, a nurse at King Edward VII Hospital in London, had been converted at All Souls and joined Frances's beginners group. She later studied at Ridgelands Bible College, while she explored the possibility of overseas service, then used her nursing skills at Monkton Combe Junior School in Bath. She and Frances were good friends over many years. Meg died very suddenly in 1998, having left a gift for Frances in her Will; this would be used to subdivide the loft space into two bedrooms, both en suite.

The Hookses gradually expanded to a total of sixteen rooms, and a Management Committee was appointed to have oversight. Frances the Omnicompetent brought a creativity to its furnishing and its soft furnishing. She was to make all the curtains, a task largely completed at weekends. This was her first attempt at curtain-making, learning along the way. John Stott took particular interest in all aspects of The Hookses, and Frances brought swatches of curtain material for him to look at, knowing his preference for bright colours. She and her friend Vivienne Curry went shopping for furniture in Heal's in Tottenham Court Road. With furniture as with bedding, crockery and saucepans, the key was good quality, but not extravagance. Having grown up in the country, Frances loved going to The Hookses, and for years took responsibility for closing the house down in the Autumn and opening it again in the Spring, driving over to Pembrokeshire with two or three friends to help her. This, like so much else, was a labour of love.

In April 1992, John Stott and Toby Howarth with help from Andrew and Elizabeth Scott, two friends from All Souls, worked to lay a thirty-foot-long walkway outside Frances Whitehead's office in The Hermitage. It was built, said John, so that 'Frances won't get her feet wet in winter'. As an evident mark of his appreciation, and with a touch of boyish spirit, he named it, 'The Frances Whitehead 36th anniversary walkway', that is counting the years from April 1956 when she began as church secretary.[70] A small ceremony was staged to mark its official opening, with Frances cutting an improvised ribbon, and receiving a presentation from the Scotts' small daughter, Sally.

In 2001 John Stott marked his eightieth birthday. In celebration of this event, he agreed that supporters of Langham Partnership be invited to make a gift to the ministry. In due course he was persuaded that part of the money should be used for improving The Hermitage 'for his successor'. (This approach was Frances's idea, for he would have been very reluctant to agree, had it been for himself.) The architect would be David Gallagher from All Souls. This marked the start of a good friendship between David and Frances, as she handled most of the detail.[71]

Typing manuscripts

Frances's main work at The Hookses was focused on typing Stott's manuscripts. While she typed all the books Stott authored, her support also extended to the books he edited. Here her contribution lay largely in correspondence. John Stott was New Testament Editor of the *Bible Speaks Today* series, and would read each manuscript assiduously and correspond with its author. More, he worked to edit all the papers from a series of consultations arranged by the Lausanne Movement.[72] Here was some of the sharpest thinking the evangelical church had to offer, but work had to be done to make the papers lucid, and flowing. The genius of Lausanne was to bring together evangelical leaders from across the world, and the majority were not first-language English speakers. Stott was a skilled editor, and the fruit of his labours was clear to see, but at no small cost for this pressured two-man team.

As well as typing books, she endeavoured to keep up with other tasks too, as the backlog when they returned to Weymouth Street could otherwise be fearful. Familiar with John Stott's contractions of words and phrases, she converted his longhand into typescript at a pace, then passed the typed copy back to him for, in his expression, 'titivation'. Occasionally she would need to retype some pages, if he wanted to insert extra text. All Stott's books had been through several stages before the final manuscript was written. They had often begun as a lecture series in the All Souls Bible School, then been reworked, and preached, first in All Souls then in other contexts around the world. So by the time the material was worked into a book, it had been processed and refined over several years.[73]

Sunday Worship and a broken vow

Philip Billson, a BBC Producer of Radio 4's *Sunday Worship*, had long appreciated John Stott's work. It had been an ambition of his to create a worship service with John as preacher, in which listeners could benefit from his love of the natural world, and of seeing God's presence in it. Stott suggested that this be recorded at The Hookses. With Nick Page, a former member of All Souls, as presenter, and with participation from Frances, Matthew Smith and Dennis Wight, the vicar at Dale, this was recorded just outside the Hermitage study window. The theme was borrowed from the words of Martin Luther, the sixteenth century Reformer: 'Let the little birds be your theologians'. The half-hour programme was beautifully crafted, with conversation, readings and prayer. Fittingly, the hymns came from the Welsh Baptist choir; George Beverley Shea – who had sung at many of Billy Graham's crusades, including the one at Haringay; and the All Souls choir and orchestra. The service closed with Timothy Dudley-Smith's hymn 'Lord, for the Years'.

The young girl from Summerside House had vowed in her Malvern days never to speak in public again, but was now to break that vow. The terrifying ordeal of addressing a group of pupils and staff in her school House would be forgotten as she sat looking out over the familiar bay, and read scripture from Jeremiah 8:4-7 and Matthew 6:25. The programme was to be broadcast on 18 April 2004 to an audience of over one-and-a-half million.

The spiritual, the practical, the humorous

The Hookses would always bring together the spiritual and the practical; the idyll of the setting and the hard work which accompanies all country living. Having grown up in Beara, the daily work of looking after ponies and helping with the fruit picking was part of life. Learning practical skills from her father, and the adventures of her travels in South Africa, meant Frances was used to hard work, and practically-minded.

Describing times at The Hookses from the vantage point of a Study Assistant, Matthew Smith recalls 'a productive rhythm, with most of the time set aside for work, but other times for [the happy triumvirate] to be together – breakfast, lunch, afternoon tea on the terrace, dinner, followed by a storybook and then Bible study. Sometimes Uncle John would read to Frances and me from what he had written that day. On other occasions, he would read from Saki, which would sometimes leave the three of us in fits of laughter!'

In December 2005, after major renovations at The Hookses, it was Frances who drove down to Pembrokeshire to inspect the property and prepare a snagging report, which was comprehensive, detailed and technical. Blotchy walls, cracked plaster, electrical problems, potential plumbing problems, uneven flagstones, ventilation problems, inaccessible plug points, sensors needed, cowl on top of boiler flu to be replaced. Further, she noted that some 'yellowish cement or plaster' had been thrown against the cliff face and looked unsightly. The door jambs needed to be made good on the woodshed and the tool shed; the driveway repaired. And a new shed was needed behind the house to store the terrace furniture.

While The Hookses provided John Stott with a writing retreat, it also provided space to entertain friends. While he and Frances would always use significant time to work, there were often old friends there with them, enjoying a holiday and making for fine, and often hilarious, company.

John Smith, Matthew Smith's father, had spent five years in the Wreckage, and over the years which followed, Frances was to become a friend of the whole Smith family. John and his wife, Anna, with Matthew and his brother Nathan, were regular visitors at The Hookses, and Frances spent time in the Smiths' home in Bristol. John Smith recalled of John Stott that he was 'the ever-able raconteur, always with a feast of stories to tell, both true and apocryphal, causing much mirth. Some of these anecdotes had been told before, but Frances would mostly claim she had 'never heard that one!'

Frances's systems of guarding the Rector in the days of the Wreckage had not been foiled by John Smith, despite his imaginative attempt with the help of David Wells. However, John Smith was not to be beaten, and he retained Frances in his sights for further fun at her expense. Her pronunciation, not unlike that of John Stott, could not pass without notice. He recalls:

Tolerance was another of Frances' qualities. She was sometimes the victim of some inane teasing on my part. I used to ask her if, when she retired, she would speak less quickly, but it never happened. Then I tried this:

Me:	'How do you pronounce O R F, Frances?'
Frances:	'Orf'
Me:	'How do you pronounce O F F, Frances?'
Frances:	'Off'
Me:	Then why do you usually pronounce O F F Orf?'

She treated such nonsense, as did Uncle John, indulgently and with a good measure of tolerance.

John Smith took liberties others didn't, but Frances gave as good as she got. In Stott's final trip to The Hookses in 2008, as so often before, a small group of friends were also invited. Frances, aged eighty-two, retained the same dominant streak in her personality which she had shown throughout, from her days in the Wreckage. It was unlikely to change now. 'Frances – you are *bossy!*' said John Smith on one occasion. Others seemed a little taken aback at his remark, which seemed inappropriate to a woman of her age. They wondered how she would respond. No concern was necessary. 'Yes, I know,' she reposted. 'But I am praying about it.'

CHAPTER TWELVE
Lambeth Palace, 24 July, 2001

The Archbishop of Canterbury confers degrees each year at the discretion of an advisory group. This tradition dates back to the Ecclesiastical Licences Act of 1533, instituted by Henry VIII, while in the process of breaking from Rome. These are not 'honorary degrees' as usually understood, though most are conferred solely on the discretion of the Archbishop and his advisors. By contrast, they are considered to be earned degrees.

John Stott was given a DD in 1983. He already had honorary doctorates from universities, but these are generally not used outside the walls of the conferring Institution. From now on, he would use the title, conferred as earned, in recognition of the scholarship he had brought to the church.

In 2000, Stott had been asked to write a reference in support of a nomination received by the Archbishop, for Frances Whitehead to receive a Lambeth MA. He was delighted to learn that she had been nominated for this honour. He handwrote his reference (as Frances could not be asked to type it), with a photocopy carefully retained in his flat, and put the envelope in the post box. This nomination would not guarantee that Frances would be selected for the degree, so he kept the matter confidential. Frances was by this time aged seventy-five, but still working four days a week.

John Stott set out a brief record of Frances's background and training, and her 'extraordinary degree of faithfulness and ability'. Illustrating this, he noted the number of his books Frances had typed: 'She also reflects as she types, and raises points of grammar, accuracy or theology'.

He added 'She is thoroughly computerized. She is also very skilled with figures, and has handled the covenants (now gift aid donations) for All Souls Church, the Langham Trust and other organisations. She never seems to make a mistake.' He described her writing of Minutes as being 'with succinctness and accuracy'.

The effectiveness of Stott's growing role internationally had depended much on Frances, and on her grasp of situations in which he would be ministering, so she could respond to questions from hosts and handle follow-up correspondence. His reference for her continued in the third person:

> **Wider Horizons:** John Stott's overseas correspondence and travel have brought Frances into touch with Xtn [sic] leaders in many other countries, where she is widely and affectionately known as 'Auntie Frances'. People might fax or phone her from all over the world, asking for information or advice. She has been a Trustee of the Evangelical Literature Trust and a member of the Langham Trust Scholarship Committee, both in her own right, and has contributed helpfully to the discussions.
>
> She went in 1980 to the Lausanne Consultation on World Evangelization in Pattaya, Thailand, and gave secretarial assistance. She has a particular concern for worldwide mission, serves on the All Souls World Focus (*ie* mission) committee, and has an intimate knowledge of All Souls missionaries.
>
> **Her Intellectual Capacity:** Frances is gifted as a teacher, and for 40 years has led one of the 'fellowship groups' at All Souls Church. She is an avid reader, especially of theological and biographical books.
>
> John Stott has often described Frances as 'omnicompetent'. Her Xtn dedication is beyond praise. He could not possibly have continued in his multifarious commitments (travel, writing, preaching and lecturing) without her support and encouragement.
>
> Finally, Frances is extremely intelligent. Given the opportunity, she could easily have become a university graduate.[74]

Stott then added a personal note at the bottom to the Archbishop. He explained that it had not been his idea to nominate Frances for consideration as a possible candidate for a Lambeth degree, saying 'I wish it had been!' for the nomination had his wholehearted support.

Traditionally, Archbishops would use their own university, generally Oxford or Cambridge, through which to confer this degree. George Carey had not been through a traditional university education before training for the ministry at St John's College, Nottingham. So he adopted Oxford as his university, and Frances would be hooded in the red silk of its Masters degree. Lambeth degrees have historically been awarded in Divinity, Law, Arts, Literature, Medicine, and Music.

Early in the New Year of 2001, Frances received the invitation from Lambeth Palace. She responded on her own letterhead:

> From Frances Whitehead
> (Secretary to John Stott)
> 12 Weymouth Street
> London W1N 3FB
> 8 February 2001

The Most Rev Dr George Carey
Archbishop of Canterbury
Lambeth Palace
London
SE1 7JU

Dear Archbishop George

Your kind letter of January 30 has quite taken my breath away! Thank you so much for it. I apologise for the delay in replying, but I was so astonished by what you say about conferring a Lambeth degree on me, that I really did not know how to respond!

However, having now had time to consider this honour, I would like most gratefully to accept it, although I feel very unworthy of receiving a degree for which I have not had to do the appropriate academic work. But I feel very privileged that you should have considered me for this award and shall look forward to the ceremony on June 21.

With renewed gratitude for your kind thoughtfulness.

Yours very sincerely

Frances Whitehead

The news was announced in All Souls at John Stott's eightieth birthday celebration. It was a wonderful recognition of the way she had enriched and expanded John's ministry, and was greeted with spontaneous applause and a standing ovation. Frances received the degree of MA (Cantuar) on 24 July, 2001. She never found out who nominated her for it.

Frances duly donned the Oxford MA gown and joined a group of fifteen other men and women receiving degrees that day in the Palace Chapel. In alphabetical order, each was called to stand while their citation was read. Then each knelt at the rail and received a hood from the Archbishop. Frances was last. As she stood up and returned to her seat, she smiled with joy. John commented afterwards that she was the only one who smiled.

Her citation read:

> **GEORGE LEONARD** by divine Providence **LORD ARCHBISHOP OF CANTERBURY**, Primate of all England and Metropolitan, by Authority of Parliament, lawfully empowered for the purposes herein written: **To** our beloved in Christ **FRANCES WHITEHEAD health and grace** in Jesus Christ our Saviour
>
> **WHEREAS** in Schools regularly instituted, the Laudable Usage and Custom hath long prevailed and that with the Approbation as well of the pure Reformed Churches as of the most learned Men for many Ages past, that they who have with Proficiency and Applause exerted themselves in the Study of any liberal Science, should be graced with some eminent Degree of Dignity:
>
> **AND WHEREAS** the Archbishops of Canterbury, enabled by the public Authority of the Law, do enjoy, and long have

enjoyed, the Power of conferring Degrees and Titles of Honour upon those considered deserving of such recognition as by an Authentic Book of Taxations of Faculties are confirmed by Authority of Parliament, doth more fully appear:

WE THEREFORE, being vested with the Authority aforesaid, and following the example of our predecessors, in recognition of your energetic and enthusiastic ministry to God's Church through your dedicated support of Doctor John Stott for over forty years and for your visible Christian witness, have judged it expedient that you whose Uprightness of Life, Sound Doctrine, and Purity of Morals, are manifest unto Us, be dignified with the Degree of **MASTER of ARTS**

AND WE do by these Presents, so far as in Us lies, and the Laws of this Realm do allow, accordingly create you an actual **MASTER of ARTS**

AND WE do also admit you into the number of the Masters of Arts of this Realm: the Oath here under written having been by Us or Our Master of the Faculties first required of you, and by you duly taken and subscribed

I, FRANCES WHITEHEAD the Person to be admitted to the Degree of Master of Arts by the Most Reverend Father in God, **GEORGE LEONARD** by Divine Providence, Lord Archbishop of Canterbury, Primate of all England, and Metropolitan, do swear by Almighty God that I will be faithful and bear true Allegiance to **HER MAJESTY QUEEN ELIZABETH THE SECOND**, Her Heirs and Successors, according to Law

PROVIDED ALWAYS that these Presents do not avail you anything, unless duly registered by the Clerk of the Crown in Chancery

GIVEN under the Seal of Our **OFFICE OF FACULTIES** at **WESTMINSTER** this **twenty-fourth** day of **July** in the Year of Our Lord Two Thousand and One and in the **Eleventh** Year of our Translation

P F Beesley **REGISTRAR**

Lambeth Palace stands on the south bank of the Thames, slightly to the east of the Palace of Westminster and the Houses of Parliament. Lambeth has been a bishop's palace since the thirteenth century. John Stott, Corey Widmer and his wife Sarah, Rose McIrath, Timothy and Arlette Dudley-Smith, Vivienne Curry, Mary Collins, a schoolteacher friend, and Mary Stopps (whom we meet in the next chapter), accompanied Frances for this special recognition. Mary Collins had just been given the headship of a Church of England primary school in Twickenham. Frances was so pleased to learn this news that John Stott quipped that he felt Frances was more excited about Mary's promotion than about her own graduation.

CHAPTER THIRTEEN
Bourne End: 1971 onwards

Sylvia Dunsford died in 1971, and Evelyn Whitehead returned permanently to England.

Evelyn and Sylvia had spent some years back in the UK from the late 1950s, when Evelyn's mother, Beatrice, started to become frail. Their first house was in Brockenhurst, in the New Forest, which they nicknamed 'green hell' because of its overwhelming trees and shrubs. Soon they moved to another, near Beaulieu. Frances kept in touch and often visited them. In the early 1960s they took a flat in Torquay, to be nearer Beatrice Eastley. When Beatrice died in 1965, Evelyn and Sylvia moved back to the Continent, settling first on the French Riviera.

By the time Sylvia died, they were living in Bordighera on the Italian Riviera, where Sylvia had a cousin. When news arrived of Sylvia's death, Frances drove over to Italy, helped her mother with the folding up of affairs, and brought her mother back to London. Evelyn stayed temporarily with Frances's friend Shelagh Brown,[75] then with Frances, while they house-hunted each weekend in the home counties. Their plan was to buy a house to share, west of London, so Frances could make an easy escape on Friday evenings, to join her mother for weekends.

It was an unusual set of circumstances. Evelyn Whitehead was an independent-minded woman. Her marriage to Claude Whitehead had lasted only a few years before it began to show signs of strain. Frances grew up feeling very close to her father. They had spent much time together, and their father–daughter bond was made all the stronger by the untimely loss of Pamela followed by her mother leaving home. While Frances as a young adult had travelled with Evelyn and Sylvia first to Switzerland and then to South Africa, the bond between them was never deep. The two older women shared a friendship which, while purely platonic, remained exclusive. So, when Evelyn moved back to England and she and Frances shared a home, they did not communicate on a deep level.

Finding a home

Finding a home which would work well for both of them took time. Eventually in 1973, they moved to Bourne End in Buckinghamshire. This large village sits between the M4 and M40 motorways, at the intersection of the River Wye and the Thames. It takes its name from its location at the end of the Wye, 'bourne' being an Old English word for river. Bourne End was home for several years, from 1929, to the children's writer Enid Blyton, whose daughters were born there. For Frances, its pace of life provided a welcome change from working in London; it had good local shops in an attractive High Street, a library, community centre and railway station.

Frances's mother had cousins in Beaconsfield, just a few miles way, unmarried twin sisters known locally as 'the Miss Eastleys'. They were close in age, just a year apart, and Evelyn had lived near them in Bovey. They did not share a great deal in common with Evelyn, but family bonds run deep, and Evelyn was appreciative of their company and companionship. The Miss Eastleys were from a keen tennis-playing branch of the family, and had a sister who was a Wimbledon coach. Frances herself had been coached by her, though she never managed to play at a higher level than the third couple in the Malvern College first six.

The house into which the Whiteheads moved, half a mile from the village centre, was part of a large timbered Victorian building, 'Abbeymead,' tastefully converted into five homes. A sun room overlooked a private garden which attracted much birdlife. The sitting room, with its black beams against a white ceiling, would provide fitting ambience for Eastley and Whitehead furniture and paintings. It was to prove worth the wait. Frances would drive from her London flat to Bourne End on a Friday evening, arriving in time for a late supper with her mother; then return to London on Sunday afternoon, in time for the evening service at All Souls. While her mother took charge of all the cooking and cleaning, Frances would use the weekends to keep the garden in order. Evelyn Whitehead was an accomplished cook and loved the chance to entertain Frances's friends for a weekend away from London. Grace Jackson recalls spending weekends there, and Mrs Whitehead's welcome.

This home, to which Frances would eventually retire in 2011, was to reflect much of her life and history. A portrait of the young lieutenant Francis Maguire[76] hung on the wall with some Eastley miniatures, and a watercolour by Claude Hay. Three carved wooden chests, familiar from Beara days, graced the home, standing in the entrance, the sitting room and on the landing. A fine chest of drawers from the Italian Riviera was found in the sitting room, acquired by Evelyn Whitehead, and brought over from the Continent; on top of this sat a painted Chinese bowl, in which Frances's great-grandfather, the surgeon Francisco de Fernandez, and Florence Nightingale washed their hands as they scrubbed up for surgery in the Crimea.

When Frances had professed faith in Christ, in her late twenties, Evelyn Whitehead had been moved, and perhaps sensed more deeply for herself a human need for transcendence, for a relationship which is higher than human friendship. But her close bond with Sylvia Dunsford since Frances's childhood was bound to have a lasting effect on the way they related. Pamela's death had shaken Evelyn, and while she never lost her faith entirely, she had not been to church for many years, other than occasionally at Christmas and Easter. Frances would accompany her to church in Bourne End on these Festivals, though All Souls would remain Frances's own church until 2011 when she moved from London permanently.

Rose McIlrath would sometimes visit Mrs Whitehead in Bourne End while in London on business, when Frances was at The Hookses.[77] On one such visit, Evelyn spoke of her guilt at leaving Frances's father. It came out of the blue, and evidently from deep in her heart. It must have helped that now, decades later, Evelyn, a homemaker and a good cook, could in practical ways express her love, by providing a home for Frances at weekends. For Frances, who had a very forgiving nature, those years at Bourne End compensated for the decades when she could not enjoy her mother's company without Sylvia. It was a time of healing.

Evelyn was often concerned that her daughter was being over-worked by John Stott, to whom she never really warmed. Perhaps she always remained a little over-awed by him; perhaps she felt that her daughter's gifts were not being used. Evelyn's perspective of Frances's work would necessarily have been limited, for she could not have grasped the full extent of its spiritual significance, nor its global reach. While Frances sometimes referred self-deprecatingly to being 'only a typist', her mother may have felt this was true. And when Frances heaved sacks of potatoes into the car from the local Farm shop, or took John's shoes to the cobblers at the weekend, it could have appeared that he was taking advantage of her good nature. 'Surely that man can afford another pair of shoes!' she would sigh.[78]

Evelyn remained energetic, and in good health, but when she reached her early-mid nineties, it was felt that she shouldn't be left alone during the week. Frances sought advice locally about whom to approach, and was advised to contact Mary Stopps, a highly-regarded district nurse who had recently retired. Frances enquired as to whether Mary could visit Evelyn each day. Mary, originally from County Down, would become a good friend of both Evelyn and Frances. The Stoppses' home in Woburn Green was soon a regular feature of Saturday morning life for Frances, as she would call in for coffee on her way home from shopping. Through these Saturday visits, she got to know Mary's daughter Colleen, a freelance gardener. Colleen, like her mother, was to become a good friend, and would help Frances regularly with her garden, and in later years with jobs inside her home. It was around this time that Colleen took responsibility for the garden at St Teresa's Roman Catholic Church in nearby Beaconsfield, where G K Chesterton had been a prominent member.[79] To save confusion when talking with friends or family, Colleen would refer to its priest as Father Francis, and to Frances Whitehead as 'Lady Frances'.

Frances's mother dies

To mark her ninetieth birthday in 1987, Frances's mother purchased a new car, and she continued driving for several more years.

In 1996, at the age of ninety-eight, it became clear that Evelyn would benefit from the support of residential care and Frances explored a range of possible options. She found a small residential home near the river at Maidenhead where Evelyn celebrated her hundredth birthday, and eventually died in her sleep on 5 June, 2002, the day after the Queen's Golden Jubilee celebrations. John Stott took her funeral at Amersham, and her ashes were scattered above the crematorium, under a tree at the top of the hill. She was four months short of her 105th birthday. It was a peaceful end to a long life spanning three centuries.

Frances's 80th birthday

Three years later, in early 2005, as Frances approached her eightieth birthday, which would fall on Easter Day, Rose McIlrath received a call from John Stott in her Antrim home. Could she let him know when she would next be in London, as he wanted to arrange a meeting of a few friends to discuss how to mark Frances's next milestone. Not long afterwards Rose was in London on business and came to stay with Frances in Devonshire Close. Frances was a little mystified the following day that both Stott and his Study Assistant Matthew Smith were out of the office with no explanation. John had drawn together a small group of Frances's close friends – Rose, Vivienne Curry, Richard Bewes – at All Souls, to discuss plans away from Weymouth Street. The idea was conceived for Frances and Rose to spend ten days in Bruges. But first there would be a meal on 30 March at the Royal China Restaurant on Baker Street. Again care was taken over the planning, and John and Matthew made an advance visit to meet the head waiter, and to view the private room where the party would eat. An invitation was sent to a dozen of Frances's close friends, including Grace Jackson, and Mary and Colleen Stopps. There would first be a drinks reception at St Paul's, Robert Adam Street, at noon, for the party to greet Frances and one another in a leisurely way, and then they would move to the restaurant.

When the time came for the trip to Bruges, John Stott accompanied Frances and Rose to Waterloo Station. He had previously told Rose not to change any money, and now he handed them each an envelope containing a wodge of euros. 'These,' he said 'are so you can treat each other.' As they watched him leave, now frail and becoming a little uncertain of his steps, they were touched that he should have insisted on seeing them off, and by his generosity.

It was a memorable trip with time to visit the ancient port, and the 14th century art in the Groeningemuseum; to stroll the canals in this 'Venice of the north'; to watch the lacemaking; and to peruse the markets. They visited Flanders Field with its cemetery, war museum and dug-out trench, which brought poignant memories for Frances, whose two uncles had died at the Somme.

A telephone call heralds new decisions

On Sunday morning, 20 August, 2006, Frances was packing her car in Bourne End, ready to drive down to The Hookses. Eighty-five year-old John Stott and Chris Jones ('CJ'), his Study Assistant, would be joining her later that day, leaving London after John had preached at the 11.30 service at All Souls. She was just about to lock her front door when the telephone rang. Frances picked up the phone and heard CJ's voice. John had fallen in his flat, and was now in A&E at University College Hospital. So please would Frances drive straight there instead. A few minutes later, and Frances would already have left for West Wales. She called Rose with the news, then drove to London. John Stott had tripped over a chair, fallen, and fractured his hip.

Once discharged from hospital in London, he spent some time of convalescence in Burrswood, a Christian hospital in Kent. Sheila Moore, a member of All Souls, and a physiotherapist at Burrswood, visited John in his room one afternoon. He was delighted to talk with her, and asked if she would give him physiotherapy when he returned to London. When Frances arrived a little later, John told her that Sheila had come 'like a helicopter from heaven!' to see him through his rehabilitation.

While John was able to return to Bridford Mews, the fall would of necessity bring changes. An earlier fall at The Hookses in 2003 had landed John in hospital and caused him to miss a major trip to the US, but this fall would mark the end of an epoch. Those close to Stott would indeed refer to two epochs in Stott's later years, with 20 August 2006 as the dividing line. With dry theological wit, these were named 'before the Fall' and 'after the Fall'.

It soon became clear after his return to London that John Stott would no longer be able to manage on his own. His flat was high up in the building, and spread over two floors; and there was no space for a stairlift to be added to the spiral staircase leading up to his sitting room, nor indeed for any material changes to be made. His closest advisors – Frances and a small group from All Souls which included Chris Wright, David Turner and John Wyatt, agreed that he should be persuaded to move into residential care.[80] Having spent his whole life in London W1, and worshipped at All Souls each Sunday when he wasn't away, for as long as he could remember, it would not be easy.

Frances began to look at options. She wanted to find a place where John could share fellowship with others of like mind. Dr Dundas Moore, Sheila's husband, was Chairman of the Trustees of the College of St Barnabas in Lingfield, an establishment for retired Anglican clergy, and Sheila arranged to take Frances there to see it. Frances weighed the prospect of John's being there as carefully as she could. It was forty miles from London, but had a good train service from Charing Cross, and a railway station adjacent to the College, so international visitors could reach it without difficulty. There were lovely grounds to walk in, and the staff and residents, while largely of a higher churchmanship, would provide a clear sense of Christian community.

Frances was shown a ground floor flat which was already available. It was quiet and Frances knew John would want to continue studying as long as his eyesight would allow. He had one more book to write, in his own words, 'to say goodbye' to his readers. John was prepared for the move, and at the invitation of the Warden, Frances drove him down for a preliminary visit. After lunch in the refectory, Patrick Campbell, the Warden, invited John, Frances and Sheila to his house for coffee. Would the churchmanship be difficult for John? The Warden felt it better to raise the matter squarely. 'I am happy to spend my last days with anyone who loves the Lord. That's my only criterion,' John responded. While there for a short trial stay soon afterwards, to get the feel for it, he asked his niece Caroline and one or two others to visit him. These decisions need careful thought, for the elderly and for their families and friends. It was agreed that a move to St Barnabas would prove the best way forward.

Frances drew a scaled plan on graph paper, so John could choose what furniture to take with him. She had done the same forty years earlier, when the Bridford Mews flat was completed. The desk at which he had always worked would be placed in front of the leaded window, which overlooked the corner of the quadrangle. For the walls he chose some favourite framed photographs of birds, and, not surprisingly, his framed engraving of Charles Simeon. Frances drove John down to Lingfield in her red Corsa, with a case of clothes, a full set of his published work, and some extra copies of a few titles to give away. The happy triumvirate would no longer be meeting around the breakfast table overlooking Bridford Mews.

CHAPTER FOURTEEN
John Stott finishes his race

When John Stott moved to the College of St Barnabas in July 2007, Frances and CJ, John's final Study Assistant, made arrangements for his flat to be cleared. Five years earlier, John and Frances had met with Claire Brown, the archivist at Lambeth Palace Library, and talked through the archiving of his papers – correspondence, Minutes, published work. These would go there when he died. His dining table and chairs were given to a young friend setting up home in Cambridge; his bookcases taken downstairs into the Rectory basement.

Books were sent in different directions to those who would appreciate them, and to ministries with which John had close links. At John's request, Frances and CJ shipped his bird books to Peter Harris, the Director of A Rocha, and his painting of a saddleback bird to Rick Warren at Saddleback Church in Southern California. Then, once John went to heaven, his desk at the College of St Barnabas would be shipped to Trinity Evangelical Divinity School in Deerfield, Illinois, where he had spent a sabbatical term forty years earlier, and the engraving of Charles Simeon[81] on his wall would be shipped to Mark Labberton. One sees the careful thought running through each decision.

Frances, by now aged eighty-two, was splitting her time between London and Bourne End, still working on Stott's personal correspondence and with Langham Partnership. She kept in touch with John by phone frequently and travelled down to Lingfield once a week to see him.

With difficulty, John would still complete his final book, *The Radical Disciple*, for Frances to type. Frances continued to run his diary, and to schedule appointments for visitors, as had happened for fifty years.

John used time to study as long as his eyesight allowed, and to lead a discussion group with a few residents interested in talking about issues, for as long as he had energy. While the pace was slower, there was a continued habit of his using time as effectively as he was able.

Since soon after Frances first began in her role, John Stott had written to her each Christmas, to thank her for another year of working together. He was aware of the sacrifices she had made to support his ministry so wholeheartedly, that it had been 'a life not a job', and he did not take her for granted. His final letter to her was written on 27 December 2007, with a shaky hand, short, in uncharacteristic green biro ink, and evidently reaching for words. By this stage, his sight was failing and there were crossings out and miss-spellings. This was his first Christmas at St Barnabas, and the letter was most likely the last letter he wrote himself.

> My dear Frances,
>
> I can't find words adequate to express my gratitude for all you have done for me throughout this year – especially in your weekly visit and undertaking so much in between visits. I know that I am extremely lucky to have your multifarious forms of support. I am amazed at your ability, and your willingness, to undertake so many tasks – writing my letters for me and keeping importunate persons at bay.
>
> Please forgive the spelling and other mistakes in this letter.
>
> With much love and gratitude
>
> As ever
>
> John

By early 2009, it became clear that John Stott needed more help from the nursing staff, and plans were put in place for him to move upstairs, to a large bedsitting room, where he could receive full residential care. He kept up with news from Langham Partnership and All Souls through their prayer diaries, and received a stream of regular visitors. He wrote in his last annual newsletter, in July that year 'I feel I now belong here; it is my home.' As the move upstairs was planned, Frances again created a scale plan of John's new room, this time a 3D model, so they could work out the best configurations for his furniture.

For Frances, apart from typing John Stott's final book, a further three tasks lay ahead: to fold up outstanding correspondence, to sort out the considerable accumulation of work in her office, which also stored a number of Stott's book manuscripts in long-hand; and to gather his archives for Lambeth Palace.

Over the course of 2010, and into 2011, John Stott grew progressively weaker. He was able to enjoy a celebratory tea on 27 April 2011, his ninetieth birthday, with some old friends. For this event Chris Wright had edited a final Festschrift *John Stott: A Portrait by his friends* which he dedicated to Frances. In the dedication Chris notes that without her help, 'the portrait would have looked very different'. A special tea was laid out and once the residents had gathered, John was wheeled in to be welcomed by everyone singing 'Happy Birthday'. After a brief speech by the deputy warden, a birthday cake appeared. John responded 'with a wave of his hand and the plunging of a large knife into the cake'. That was probably the last time most of the residents saw him.

John remained alert in mind and interested in any news Frances could share on her Tuesday visits, but he found speaking very tiring, and would often shut his eyes and doze. By now he was spending most of the time in bed, as sitting in a chair was too uncomfortable. He had named his two executors as his Accountant, and 'my friend, Frances Whitehead'. John had once remarked poignantly to Matthew Smith that he hoped he would die before Frances, as he was not sure how he could manage without her.

Lingfield, 27 July 2011

When Frances had visited John on the 26 July, he had been very sleepy and hardly communicated, so Frances had just sat quietly beside his bed and prayed. The following morning, soon after 7.00am, she was not surprised to receive a call from the staff of St Barnabas to say he was now failing, and might not survive the day.

Frances called Rose in Ireland with the news, and then called Matthew Smith. She arranged to travel down to Lingfield with Caroline Bowerman, John's eldest niece, who collected her from Devonshire Close. A small group would soon gather of half a dozen close friends and family. In the early afternoon, one of the group suggested they play a CD of excerpts from Handel's *Messiah*, which John's niece Sarah had left, knowing her uncle's love of it. In due course the Hallelujah Chorus completed the Second Part. Then came the confident soprano air, 'I know that my Redeemer liveth'. Soon after this John Stott entered Christ's nearer presence while the Apostle Paul's declaration could be heard: 'The trumpet shall sound, and the dead shall be raised incorruptible, and we shall be changed.'

John Stott died mid-afternoon, surrounded by some of those dearest to him. He had been a resident in St Barnabas for almost four years and won the affection of its Filipino staff, to whom, to his delight, he was *Lolo* (grandpa).

At Keswick

Chris Wright and his wife, Liz, were three hundred miles away at the annual Keswick Convention, where Chris was the week's Bible expositor. Chris recalls:

> 'Liz and I went for a cycle ride that afternoon, to a village some miles outside Keswick. Fortunately we remained within mobile phone range, for while we were having a late lunch in the village pub garden, my phone rang. It was Matthew Smith with the news that John Stott had died a few minutes earlier and the medical staff at St Barnabas had confirmed his death.
>
> After talking with Matthew, I spoke briefly with Frances. It was a moment we had all known was approaching, but it had its own unique poignancy and sacredness. It was also a moment we had long prepared for. Since his fall in 2006, we knew there would be global interest, many people to be informed, press enquiries, obituaries, etc.
>
> A small group, codenamed the 'Snowy Owl Committee' (after John Stott's legendary pursuit of the Arctic Snowy Owl), had

constructed a memorial website to go live immediately the Event happened. We had also put together a frequently-rehearsed plan of action. Frances had a key role in this, since it would be her privilege and desire to be the first to inform as many of John's friends as possible. So, before we left the pub garden, with one phone call to Ian Buchanan, then Executive Director of Langham Partnership UK and Ireland (and convenor of the Snowy Owl Committee), I set in motion a cascade of information through agreed channels.

Liz and I cycled back to Keswick as fast as we could. There I phoned Matthew again to learn a little more about the circumstances, and heard that John had died among those closest of friends, with the words of Handel's *Messiah* filling the air. Liz and I met with the Keswick Convention leaders, and it was agreed that I should announce John's death during the evening celebration. I can still hear the deep 'Oh!' of the gathering as I shared the news, with the very few words that I could control. By the time I sat down, it was being tweeted and texted worldwide – as we had expected – and emails were coming in even before we got back to our hotel after the meeting. The world knew within hours.

The Keswick leaders understood our need to return to London, to be with Frances and attend to so much. So the next morning, Thursday, it was arranged that I should video record my final Bible exposition (in a small room at the hotel, with an audience of six!), before going to the tent to deliver the one for that day. Immediately after the service, Liz and I were whisked off to the station and caught the train back to London – already dealing with an avalanche of emails.

A long time earlier Frances and I had prepared the text of the letter that we would jointly sign and send out to some two thousand people in the UK alone. By the end of the second day after John's death, that letter was dated, printed, copied on the All Souls copier, stuffed in pre-addressed envelopes by willing volunteers from the church, and delivered in batches to local post-boxes.

And that was just the start of a task that occupied the coming six months – through the funeral service at All Souls, a number of memorial and thanksgiving services, climaxing with the one at St Paul's Cathedral in January 2012. Frances, of course, carried a substantial part of that load. Frances, Liz and I wryly observed together that our beloved brother John had given us more work in death than in life!'

By late evening on Wednesday 27 July, the news of John Stott's death could be seen across the bottom of UK television screens, on the BBC ticker. Frances was unaware of this, nor was she aware of the report on the Radio 4 *Today* Programme the following morning, or the feature on the Radio 4 website, in which Billy Graham spoke of John as a friend and advisor, and said he looked forward to meeting him in heaven. Robert Piggott, the BBC Religious Affairs correspondent, paid tribute to Stott's ability to 'make complex, theological ideas easy to understand'. The UK broadsheets would all publish obituaries on Friday, 29 July, a day behind the US East Coast, where tributes appeared earlier, having the advantage of five extra hours on the day his death was announced.

There is always a gulf between the private and the public at such times; the mourning of friends and family, and the sense of loss felt more widely. For Frances, the next weeks brought the numbness of bereavement. She had seen the limitations with which John had struggled, and the particular difficulties of his last months, and was thankful that his suffering was over. She had given herself wholly to supporting his ministry since 1956, from the age of thirty-one. Now, in 2011, fifty-five years later, she was able to say she had no regrets; there was nothing unresolved; there were no 'if onlys'. While she mourned inwardly, she did not weep; for through the blur of the next months, there was always a deep sense of gratitude – for John's life, for his ministry and for his friendship.

In due course Frances's mind would turn to all that needed to be done over the next months, as the legacy of John Stott's ministry would be preserved, formally in the Lambeth Palace archive, while more widely through his Literary Executors, and through the movements he had founded or helped to shape. For now her mind was full, not of the stuff of obituaries – biographical overview, links with the Palace, numbers of books in how many languages, wide influence in the university arena or the Majority World – but of personal memories.

London, 8 August 2011

John Stott's funeral was held in a full All Souls Church on a warm, sunny morning, 8 August 2011. It was a gathering of friends, family, and church family from All Souls and from the College of St Barnabas.[82] Caroline Bowerman brought a tribute to her 'Uncle Johnnie' from the family. Frances read John 14:15-24. Chris Wright preached.

David Turner gave a tribute from the church family, combining warmth and humour.

> I shall never forget the impact of seeing John kneel to pray in the pulpit before he preached, in the scarlet cassock of a Queen's Chaplain under a gleaming white surplice. This was expository preaching of exceptional clarity and authority such as I had never heard.
>
> John treated us as intelligent people. He trained us in 'thoughtful allegiance' to scripture. He moved us by his passion. He taught us 'double listening' – the need to 'hear' the word and the world and to find the connections. He abhorred in equal measure 'undevotional theology' (mind without heart) and 'untheological devotion' (heart without mind). He was, as he liked to say, 'an impenitent believer in the importance of biblical preaching'. We loved it!
>
> Landmark sermon series here at All Souls on Romans, Ephesians, Acts, II Timothy, and on Issues Facing Christians, later travelled the world and formed the core of some of John's fifty-one books. As we read those books now, we can still hear the structure of his delivery and the cadences of his voice. We would sometimes joke that John was clearer on the Apostle Paul than was the Apostle Paul!

David Turner added poignantly, 'The glorious transcendent reality of eternal life eases the very real sense of loss we feel . . . This is, supremely, an *au revoir* occasion, and you do not need firsts in French and Theology from Cambridge to know what that means!'

Frances, John's nieces and their families, and a few close friends, then drove to the crematorium in Golders Green. After a packed service in All Souls, this was a quieter gathering. Timothy Dudley-Smith was there, Phillip and Sheila Herbert, John and Anna Smith, Chris and Liz Wright, Roy and Helen McCloughry, perhaps thirty at most. Richard Bewes took the service. Richard had known John for over sixty years, since soon after arriving in England from his childhood home in Kenya, where his parents were missionaries. It was John Stott who had driven him, as a thirteen-year-old schoolboy at Marlborough, to his first Bash camp.

Knowing the service would be a hard task emotionally, Richard scripted himself in full. He began: 'Our loving heavenly Father, we have come directly from All Souls Church to be here in the intimacy and quiet of this chapel, for this moment of committal as we lay to rest the body of John, your servant.' Then Emily Bowerman, John's great niece, read the declaratory words of the Apostle Paul in 1 Corinthians 15:50-58.

Richard Bewes based his reflections on Exodus 33, a passage he had read to John not long before, where Moses asks to see the glory of God, and his request is met, but only in part, as God places Moses in the cleft of a rock, as he passes by. Richard showed those gathered a photo of John, sitting in a cleft near The Hookses, where he had sat and reflected over many years. As the curtain was about to draw over the coffin, 'slowly and symbolically', Richard, through the scriptures, directed people's eyes beyond the mortal to the eternal.

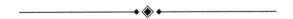

For those close to John in his ministry, this was not so much the funeral of a colleague, but of a family member; and for family members the anti-climax after the service is always palpable. Chris and Liz Wright,

JY and Corey, took Frances for tea in Villandry's on Great Portland Street, and they sat at a table on the pavement in the afternoon sun, reminiscing. Then Chris and Liz had an idea. They had champagne in their fridge waiting for an appropriate occasion, and this was the time. A phone call to Hugh and Clare Palmer, to ask if they may use the Rectory drawing room, and a couple more calls to US friends who had flown over for the funeral, put impromptu plans in place.

That evening they gathered first in the Rectory drawing room for a champagne toast, joined by the Palmers. It was over forty years since Frances had last worked at Sir Arnold's desk in the corner of the room, and 55 years since she had first started to run down the stairs to answer the front door; more than half a century had passed since Winnie was tying up and re-tying her tin of buns for the newcomers' get-togethers.

Then the party left the Rectory to take what had become a very familiar walk for John Stott with his international friends, turning left along Weymouth Street, and almost immediately left again, to a Turkish restaurant in Great Portland Street. Its senior proprietor, an elderly Turkish man, had become a personal friend of John over the years. Whenever Chris and Liz ate there with international friends, after John had moved to St Barnabas, he would ask after him, and give them a box of Turkish Delight for him. This was a chance to share memories, swap stories and celebrate friendship. Corey Widmer and JY, Fred and Nancy Gale, David Spence – all had stories to tell their British friends, and greetings to send to others. It was a happy evening of shared friendship and amusing anecdotes, of laughter, thankfulness, and Christian hope.

Dale, 4 September 2011

John Stott's Will bore instructions for his ashes to be buried in the cemetery in Dale, where they were placed beside the grave of an old friend from the village. The service for the interment at the village church, St James the Great, was at 3.00pm. Frances travelled down to Pembrokeshire the day before, with Matthew, to be joined by the Bowerman family at The Hookses.

By the time the service was to begin, the morning sunshine had given way to black clouds then torrential rain, so the eighty people filling the small church arrived with umbrellas, or with their hoods up. Frances knew most people there as members of the little parish church and the wider village community would always extend a warm welcome to The Hookses party. Indeed, Frances, John and the Study Assistants had long been adopted as part of the community.

Bill Lewis, a retired vicar from Milford Haven, one of John's oldest friends in the region, led the service, based on Evening Prayer of the Church in Wales. The thirteenth century stones echoed with Christ-centred hymns sung to great Welsh melodies: Jesu, Lover of my soul; How sweet the name of Jesus sounds; and Oh the deep, deep love of Jesus. At Stott's request, Chris Wright preached the sermon.

It was moving to see those who had come who were not members of the village church: the wife of the farmer whose sheep grazed the land surrounding The Hookses; the village plumber, who later stood alone with head bowed by the graveside paying his respects; the lady who came once a week to check the property between visiting houseparties; the widow of a builder who had helped with early work at The Hookses. Each had been touched by John Stott's life. Knowing that John would have wanted the gospel to be explained with the local community gathered, Chris read a short extract from John's book *Why I am a Christian*, describing how he first found faith in Christ while a schoolboy at Rugby. Chris commended to everyone present John Stott's own response to what he heard as a teenager. Obituaries which appeared in the national press had been passed around to read. While John Stott was regarded simply as a gracious Englishman who had come to Dale for peace and quiet to write, there had been, over the years, a growing sense of his global fame. This was a service for John Stott's Dale friends, and most had long Welsh histories. Alongside them in the congregation, as well as Frances, Liz Wright, the Smith and Bowerman families and the Herberts, was David Manohar, a Langham scholar from India, with his wife Christina. Their presence brought a symbolic reminder that the global Church was always in Stott's mind.

Chris Wright laid the casket in the ground as 'the swallows and martins twittered over our heads, the cattle grazed contentedly a few yards away, and the wind whipped in off nearby West Dale Bay'.[83]

John Stott had asked his executors that a headstone be carved out of Welsh slate, with, as stated earlier, the same epitaph as was used of his mentor Charles Simeon.[84]

The next day, Chris Wright wrote to friends and Langham Partnership supporters with his reflections. 'It seems fitting,' he said, 'for a man who, like Moses, was one of the greatest leaders God has given to his people, and yet one of the humblest men. I can think of no more appropriate place for his earthly memorial than that small corner of a tiny village cemetery in the midst of lush green fields, on the very edge of the land he loved, surrounded by birds and cattle, with ivy, wildflowers and brambles climbing over the ancient red sandstone walls on either side, and the salty wind blowing in off the ocean.'

Another milestone had now been passed. Frances would return to Weymouth Street and continue the work of completing John Stott's correspondence and archiving his papers. By now aged eighty-six and spending only two days a week in London, the task would take her several months.

All Souls Church, 27 November 2011

Exactly four months after John Stott died, a special thirty-minute service was recorded in All Souls for BBC Radio 4, to pay tribute to his ministry under God through All Souls, and around the world. It would be broadcast as *Sunday Worship* on New Year's Day, 2012. Frances drove up to London on the Saturday, ready for the recording, before the morning service. Seven years had passed since the happy triumvirate had sat around a BBC microphone at The Hookses, overlooking West Dale Bay. Philip Billson was again the Producer. Frances mounted the low platform, and stood beneath the painting of Christ which had first drawn her into the church; she placed her script on the podium and told the nation the story of how she had found faith in Christ in the early hours of New Year's Day almost sixty years earlier.

This service, led by Hugh Palmer, the Rector of All Souls, held in microcosm Stott's global ministry. In so doing it perfectly exemplified the range of work Frances had supported since she left her desk at the BBC for Sir Arnold's desk in the drawing room of 12 Weymouth Street. Hugh Palmer made reference to two of John Stott's seminal works, *Issues Facing Christians Today*, published as the London Institute for Contemporary Christianity (LICC) opened its doors in 1982; and the book John Stott always considered his best, *The Cross of Christ*, published in 1986 bearing a dedication to Frances. The eight words of the titles alone would act as shorthand for John Stott's ministry; a man who had no peer, and for whom there would be no one single successor. As well as expounding the fact of, and the meaning of, the Atonement, he had taught and written of its implications for how we should then live. He had done this on all continents, in a context of the local and the global, for Stott's ministry was 'glocal' in essence decades before the term was coined.

David Turner read the scriptures and led in prayer. Professor John Wyatt spoke of his own early encounter with John Stott's preaching:

> I started attending All Souls Church in the 1970s when I was medical student. I can still remember the impact that John Stott's preaching had on me. I was electrified as he engaged honestly and thoughtfully with the controversial issues of the day – nuclear disarmament, industrial relations, the legalisation of abortion – and showed how Christian teaching could provide relevant, practical and creative responses. I had never heard preaching like this and it left an indelible impression.

Saúl and Pilar Cruz's daughter Eidi also spoke. She and her brother had known 'El Tío Juan' (Uncle John) from childhood, as John Stott would visit the Cruz family in Mexico whenever he was able. Frances and Eidi had stood with their arms around each other at John's bedside as he died.

Poem for 'an uncle with a grandfather's face'

A few days after the BBC recording, Frances received a poem from Eidi. Having worked hard to bring together a tribute for the service, which expressed what Uncle John had meant to her and to her family, Eidi turned to poetry in Spanish, and now the lines flowed. She sent her poem to her parents, then translated it into English, and emailed the translation to Frances. Eidi's poem brought an intimate perspective from a young friend who had known Uncle John for as long as she could remember. Who else could have written of an 'Uncle who looked at me with a grandfather's face'? Frances found its perspective endearing and unique. She loved its clear hope of heaven and sensed it would be appreciated by others, if it could be published.[85]

Letters and emails

As the Autumn days grew shorter, Frances received countless letters and emails, extending appreciation for her lifelong work, and recognising her own personal sense of loss. Many letters arriving at Weymouth Street, Devonshire Close or Bourne End were of the kind normally reserved for bereaved family members. She heard from some who had been in her nursery class as far back as the 1960s. There were letters from archbishops and bishops, from leading speakers and writers, and from former members of the All Souls congregation. People referred in their letters to the way Frances had supported John and enabled his ministry, some capturing aspects of her ministry or John's which had left a deep impression. David Brock, a former All Souls fellowship group leader, with beautiful, onomatopoeic rhythm, wrote of 'the distinctive sound of his voice, caressing polysyllabic words in a special way'.

Professor David Cranston from Oxford, with his parents-in-law Dickie and Rosemary Bird, was a regular visitor to The Hookses. His mother had died just a few weeks earlier. In his letter to Frances he recalled his early morning cups of tea with John when he convalesced in their home after a fall in 2002, and his conversations with him about death in his final weeks on earth. He wrote, surely speaking for many:

'And Frances, we remember you with your thoughts at this time. All that you have enabled John to do on a global scale over the last 60 years. The Christian world owes you a debt of gratitude that it will never be able to repay, and will never fully understand until glory. Thank you from one individual!'

A near contemporary of John Stott and a fellow evangelical wrote to Frances, again with touching memories. While ministering largely in the north, he had kept in touch with John, though not seen him often. 'The only thing that baffled me about John was that he finished up in the Anglo-Catholic St Barnabas.' Over the years that John was in St Barnabas, he had, his old friend continued, received four appeal letters from the College, all of which mentioned John's name as a resident. 'Clearly to have the Pillar of the Reformed and Evangelical establishment concluding his life in an Anglo-Catholic institution was important to them. It was a bit like hearing that Billy Graham had been received into the Catholic Church.' He was understandably intrigued, as others had been. 'Knowing John, I was just interested in his end-of-life change of heart.' Frances was glad to be able to reassure this old friend that John Stott had retained his firm evangelical convictions with no change of heart. While the churchmanship of St Barnabas was indeed higher than John's, he had nonetheless appreciated the Christian care he had received.

Preparing the archives

Now Frances would gather together John Stott's substantial body of correspondence, with senior figures in the church and in society, and with many, many lesser-known men and women. The archive at Lambeth would receive complete sets of Minutes of several initiatives like the National Evangelical Anglican Congresses (NEAC), the Evangelical Fellowship in the Anglican Communion (EFAC), the Evangelical Literature Trust (ELT), which was by now part of Langham Partnership, and of the London Institute for Contemporary Christianity (LICC). To these were added file copies of all the *All Souls* magazines; and the annual newsletters which had been sent to a thousand personal friends around the world. Memories! The newsletter itself was no small undertaking. Frances would add a design element by inserting photographs or graphics, arrange the printing, and then enlist the help of a working party to stuff envelopes for the mailing. The envelopes then had to be sorted into batches for the various geographical posting bands. No task in Weymouth Street had been simple. Relating to a global church always ensured that.

Frances resolved to offer a complete set of Stott's books to Ridley Hall in Cambridge, his Alma Mater, named after the great Reformer Nicholas Ridley. These were warmly accepted, with news of plans for the Hall to build a new development onsite. Its centrepiece would be its auditorium, to be named the John Stott Auditorium, in honour of the young ordinand who had trained there in the war years. Ridley had recently opened a Simeon Centre, for it was Charles Simeon who first pioneered the idea of ministerial training. Having been born one hundred and sixty-two years apart and fifty miles apart, these two kindred spirits would now both be remembered in the same Hall, in the Fenland town where they had both studied.

Frances Whitehead steadily worked through the archiving, drawer by drawer, shelf by shelf, box by box. She had retained a file copy of each of John Stott's published works, and file copies of series of articles, in the large cupboard in her office. Several of his longhand manuscripts were also there (some having been given to his former Study Assistants over the years). It would take Frances a year to complete her work in Weymouth Street. The Archives filled sixty-two boxes, all to be shipped to Lambeth Palace Library. Each of the Lambeth boxes represented a tranche of Stott's ministry, and of her work to enable it to happen, under God.

PART V

Frances Whitehead's Final Years (2011-2019)

CHAPTER FIFTEEN

Frances Whitehead's final years

Frances remained actively engaged into her early nineties. Dressed in smart casual clothes, with her hair well cut, she welcomed many visitors. For forty years and more she wore a silver medallion of St Francis around her neck – a pendant given her by Dee Dee MacLean, founding board member of Langham Partnership in the USA.

Frances showed the clear marks of being her father's daughter. All her life she followed sport, and continued to enter into the excitement and tension of the game on television, whether cricket, football, rugby, tennis, snooker or equestrian events.[86] Saturday morning coffee with Colleen Stopps in Woburn Green remained in the diary each week for as long as Frances could drive. Here Frances and Colleen, who also followed sport closely, shared their reactions to the week's events, their personal news and concerns – and laughter was never far away.

The natural world offered Frances the same interest it had since childhood, its flora and its fauna. Frances followed domestic and international affairs in the media; and she continued to read, especially, as we have learned, biographies and theology. The crossword in the daily newspaper was taken as a personal challenge for which she would enlist help over the phone, or even from strangers in a waiting room; a well-worn dictionary and Thesaurus always lay within reach. She did not like to be beaten by a crossword, or indeed by a jigsaw puzzle. Every Saturday over many years, she and Rose McIlrath each worked on *The Times* crossword, and in the evening they would try to complete it over the phone. It became a ritual for them.

Correspondence continued with many younger friends by email, including former Study Assistants; Frances's energetic and engaging mind, following trends in thinking, made for little awareness of their difference in age. She was always pleased to hear news by phone and email, and to follow with interest the arrival of new generations of children. One such arrival was baby Joshy, born in New York in 2017, the son of Matthew Smith and Eidi Cruz-Valdivieso, who were married in 2014.

As good health cannot be taken for granted, the completion of the first edition of Frances's biography was brought forward, and its launch, originally planned for Frances's ninetieth birthday, took place in All Souls in September 2014. Frances, Rose, and Colleen drove down from Bourne End. This would prove to be Frances's final visit to All Souls.

It was a very happy occasion. She and the author were interviewed in the 11.30am service by Hugh Palmer, and the book was launched in the Waldegrave Hall afterwards, with balloons and cake, and a short address from Timothy Dudley-Smith. There was a festive air to the occasion and it was followed by lunch in Weymouth Street, hosted by Hugh and Clare Palmer in the Rectory drawing room, where Frances had first worked at Sir Arnold's desk.

Having been a part of All Souls for so many years, with its expository preaching and fine music, it wasn't going to be easy for Frances to make a transition to a small parish church. From her retirement up to the age of 90, she worshipped at St John the Baptist in the adjacent village of Little Marlow, and was a member of one of its home groups. She also took part in a small fortnightly ladies' Bible study in nearby Marlow. However All Souls had probably spoilt her when it came to more parochial fare, and by the time she was ninety she felt, understandably, less and less inclination to go out.

Moving into her 90s

As Frances neared her ninetieth birthday, she started to get more tired, and was no longer able to keep up with email.[87] At Colleen's suggestion, she began to have *The i*[88] delivered every morning, so she could continue to follow current affairs, and do the crossword.

Rico Tice, from the staff at All Souls, had kept in touch with Frances, and knew she was finding it less easy to get out to church. She drew much on her personal daily Bible reading, which had been consistent throughout her life since soon after she professed faith in Christ.

Rico asked two friends in the area if they would call in on her as they were able, to give her spiritual encouragement. Jane Chaffey was the school chaplain at Wycombe Abbey, and Heidi Cooper lived locally with her family in Cookham outside Maidenhead. On one occasion Frances heard Jane's husband Jonathan, then serving as Chaplain-in-Chief of the Royal Air Force, preach at Little Marlow. Jonathan was delighted to hear that he reminded Frances of John Stott – until it transpired that this was due only to his wearing the red cassock of a Queen's Honorary Chaplain!

Heidi came from Cape Town, which Frances knew from her time in South Africa. Jane and Heidi visited consistently from then until Frances died, and would read the Bible and pray with her.

Jane regularly enquired whether she would like to take communion at home. She invariably declined the offers however, jovially playing along with being teased about backsliding, and it was clear that her own reading and praying, along with recollections of John's teachings and familiar sayings, were sustenance enough. Certainly, those who visited Frances found their times together both encouraging and enriching.

Frances would sometimes spend Christmas with the Chaffeys and their daughters. At the age of ninety she went on an Easter egg hunt in their garden, showing her playful spark and competitive spirit. She slipped on the grass in her attempt to win, but soon got up again, just a little shaken but completely undeterred.

While preferring to stay at home, Frances did, however, surprise Heidi one day by saying that she would like to see an art exhibition being hosted by St Mary's Church, Maidenhead, where Heidi was a member. It was to prove a particular blessing.

As they arrived at St Mary's, Frances happened across Mark Meynell, who'd been on the staff team at All Souls with her and had recently moved to the area. After a brief catch-up, she started to explore the exhibition, a collection of artworks by the Christian artist, Paul Hobbs. One of his installations, 'Holy Ground', consisted of twenty-four pairs of shoes from Christians around the world, with accompanying stories about their faith and how their belief in Christ was affecting their lives. Frances was drawn to one item: a small pair of children's leather shoes with a hole cut out at the toes, and she proceeded to read the story behind them. The shoes belonged to Greet Oosterbeek, born in the Netherlands during the German occupation in World War II. Her father died shortly after their evacuation, leaving Greet and her mother with no money or food. When Greet's feet grew too big for her shoes, her mother cut the leather to allow her feet room to grow.

In her late twenties, an employer sent Greet to London for six months, where she found herself at All Souls, and heard John Stott explain how she could become a new creation. She professed faith in Christ, and her life was changed. This was the only life story in the exhibition which mentioned John Stott; and Greet's interaction with him would have taken place while Frances and John were working together.

So on what was probably the only day Frances went out that year, she came across an old friend, and read a story about a person's life being transformed through John Stott's ministry. An encouragement to Frances, and a testimony to God's kindness.

Rose came over from County Antrim for Frances's ninetieth birthday on 27th March 2015. The date was marked by many friends, and large numbers of cards and of flowers arrived. Jane Chaffey arrived just after the flowers had been delivered, and put them all in water, using every vase and jug which could be found.

David Cranston collected Frances and Rose that afternoon, for a birthday tea hosted by James and Emma Kennedy, in the Kennedys' vicarage in the Cotswold town of Chipping Norton. Jonathan Cranston,[89] David's son, was there, as was the present author. Matthew Smith and his wife, Eidi, were also there, together with Eidi's mother, Pilar, and her brother, Saúl Junior.[90] James and Emma welcomed everyone around their large kitchen table to a sumptuous birthday tea.

The following day Colleen, together with Frances's neighbour Helen, arranged a small party in Frances's home for the Abbey Mead neighbours and one or two other local friends. The scent of the flowers filled the house for a week or more.

It was around this time that Frances's long-time neighbour and friend, Olive, discovered a stray cat who had made a home in Olive's garage. This long and sleek marmalade-coloured beast, with a languid, gentle nature was to play an important role in Frances's life in her declining years. Olive named him Ginger. Olive's own cat was less impressed and didn't make Ginger welcome. So having graduated from the garage to Olive's home, Ginger would leave after breakfast, to appear on the patio outside Frances's sun room, and spend much of the day with Frances. Having grown up with animals, Frances loved furry company. It would not have worked for Frances to keep a pet in her London flat but Ginger made up for those years. Frances adored him, and he her.

As Frances became more frail, friends came to visit her, or kept in touch by telephone. One such friend over the years was Shirley Done, who had once been a member of Frances's All Souls nursery class.[91]

Shirley visited Frances in Bourne End in 2016, and enjoyed a happy time of reminiscing. Olive dropped in, and Ginger was asleep on a bed upstairs. There was a consistency, Shirley recalled, about Frances's life, and in retirement she was still as Shirley had remembered her from long before in All Souls: warm, hospitable, and giving people her full attention. 'Nevertheless,' Shirley commented, 'I sometimes felt she had a vulnerability, often covered by personal discipline and extreme conscientiousness.'

Mary Collins would visit frequently from Hampton. She had known Frances from 1987, when she joined All Souls, and became a member of Frances's fortnightly home group. She recalls how carefully Frances prepared for the Bible studies, always using John's books ('she wouldn't dream of consulting anything else'). As they shared things for prayer, it became clear how much Frances cared for John's Study Assistants, and the church mission partners, who corresponded with her frequently. 'Folk loved her,' said Mary.

Until John left his flat in Weymouth Street in 2007, Frances would call in on a Sunday evening when she arrived from Bourne End, and they would walk down to the evening service together. John would take his seat on the left of the podium. Mary Collins would sit with Frances, saving her a place.

John's ministry, the happy triumvirate, the Hookses and All Souls had been Frances's life. It was a very absorbing life with little capacity for personal friendships, especially as she would spend weekends in Bourne End with her mother. Not having retired until the age of eighty-seven made it hard for Frances to find new purpose, or make new friends. Rico Tice's initiative in talking with Jane Chaffey and Heidi Cooper had been perceptive.

Bourne End, Spring 2019

By the autumn of 2018 it became clear that Frances would need a live-in carer, and her neighbour Viv Drake, who was a manager in the NHS, took a lead in arranging this.

Viv, who had known Frances as a neighbour for thirty years, described her as 'a strong, independent, intelligent woman, interested in everyone and everything.' Frances, she added, 'enjoyed friendship, help and respect' in the small community.

Ever independent, it was not easy for Frances to accept the idea of residential carers. The first proved most unsuitable and was asked to leave by the agency. Then Viv Drake arranged for Elizabeth Hernández from Spain to come.

Meeting Frances for the first time, even in her old age, could be intimidating. Elizabeth brought a humility in her demeanour, and from the outset their relationship was strong. Frances, proud of her Spanish ancestry, enjoyed talking with Elizabeth about it. She schooled Elizabeth not only in English pronunciation, but in received pronunciation, and she would insist that Elizabeth repeat a word several times until she got it right.

To satisfy her competitive spirit, Frances would challenge Elizabeth to Scrabble, knowing she would win by a mile. 'I'm going to beat you,' she would declare before the game started. Not only did she have a readier vocabulary, but she also had long experience of how best to use letters with double and triple points.

Sometimes Frances did not feel like getting up in the morning due to fatigue; yet if she saw Ginger outside, it was enough to change her mind and she would make her way to the stair lift, to let him in.

Frances would sometimes start to talk in French, and she tried to teach her carers some French. It was touching to hear one of the relief carers, sitting at Frances's bedside a week before she died, lament her failure to learn French vocabulary from Frances. Then an idea struck her, and she drew from her nursery rhymes, and sang *Frère Jacques* to Frances.

In May 2019 Frances had a two-week spell in hospital, with Elizabeth Hernández at her side every day, and friends visiting daily. Rose once more flew over from Northern Ireland. She was told by the doctor, as Frances's next-of-kin, that Frances's heart was becoming weak, and that she would not have long to live. Frances wanted to die at home, and Rose asked if this would be possible. A special bed would be needed and regular medical visits arranged. Within three or four days, Frances's home had been checked for its suitability and a bed positioned facing the garden. Frances then made the difficult journey home by ambulance, accompanied by Elizabeth.

'Team Frances' formed a WhatsApp group for regular updates. 'The best therapist,' wrote Elizabeth to the group, the day after Frances arrived home, as she posted a photo of Ginger, asleep on Frances's bed, with Frances's arm around him. Rose, by now back in Antrim, continued to call her each day, as she had for so many years.

Towards the end of her life, Frances opened her eyes only rarely, but remained aware of there being people with her. Over her two weeks back home, friends came often, and some of her relief carers visited her when not on duty; they had clearly been drawn to her.

Jonathan Chaffey had spoken with Frances about Charles Simeon on occasion, and Simeon's inspirational model as a preacher. Jonathan had preached from Simeon's pulpit in Holy Trinity, Cambridge, with its striking inscription from John 12.21: 'Sir, we would like to see Jesus'. Just two or three days before Frances died, Jonathan was at her bedside and commented on the silhouette of Simeon in the pulpit which hung on the wall, above the bed. While Frances's eyes remained shut, she vigorously waved her thin arm towards it, and then pointed to Jonathan – a clear exhortation to him to keep faithful in his preaching.

At the Thanksgiving service in All Souls, Heidi Cooper recalled how she had sung hymns beside Frances's bed around this time, not knowing whether Frances was awake or asleep. Then at one-point Frances raised her arm into the air, and, while unable to talk, moved her hand as if conducting the music. Her spiritual sense remained strong, despite her failing heart.

Frances died peacefully late afternoon on Saturday, 1 June. The Chaffeys visited that morning and read Psalm 27 to Frances as she slept. Emily Bowerman, John Stott's great niece, drove up from London and joined Elizabeth, and friends from All Souls arrived later. Frances had fought the good fight, finished the race and kept the faith; and now was stored up for her the crown of righteousness awarded to all those who long for Christ's appearing.

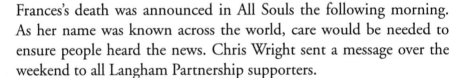

Frances's death was announced in All Souls the following morning. As her name was known across the world, care would be needed to ensure people heard the news. Chris Wright sent a message over the weekend to all Langham Partnership supporters.

That Sunday afternoon, in the small sun room of Frances's home, where she delighted in her garden, and not least in the red kites which swooped across the sky, the planning would begin for her funeral, and for a Thanksgiving service. Matthew Smith and Rose McIlrath, her executors,[92] would take the lead in making arrangements, assisted by Emily Bowerman, and the present author.[93]

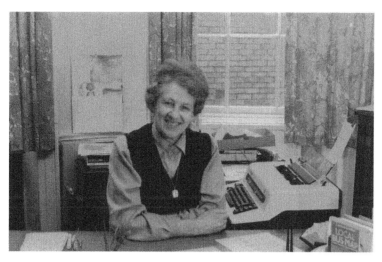

Frances at her desk in the ground-floor office.

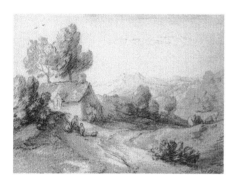 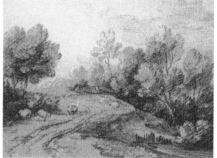

Two of the Whitehead family's Gainsborough etchings.

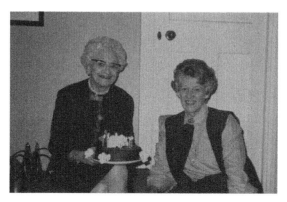

With Evelyn Whitehead in Devonshire Close on Evelyn's birthday.

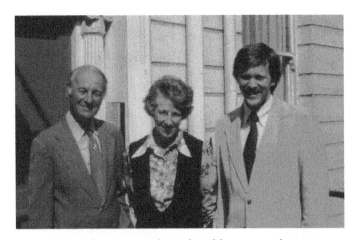

With John Stott and Mark Labberton, early 1980s.

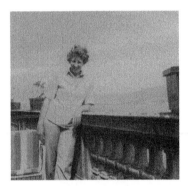 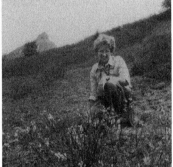

On holiday with Rose McIlrath, 1981.

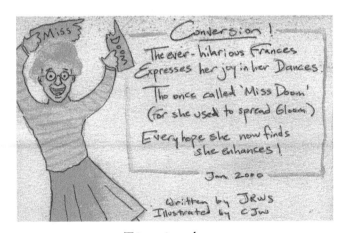

Triumvirate humour.

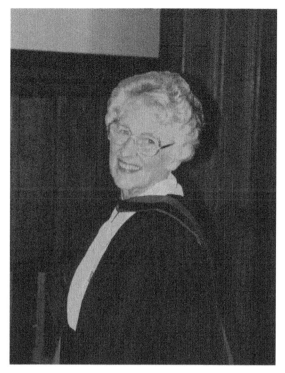

Frances with her MA (Cantuar) hood, in Oxford's red silk.

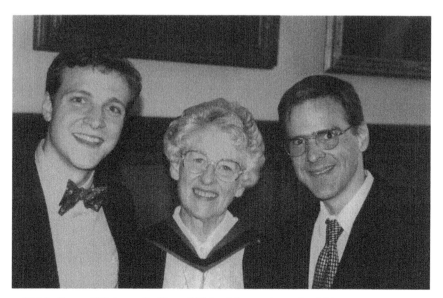

With Corey Widmer (left) and Toby Howarth at the MA ceremony, 2001.

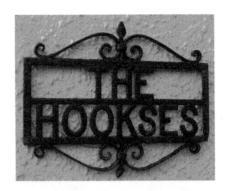

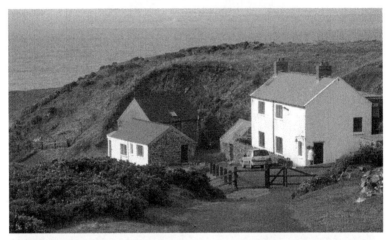

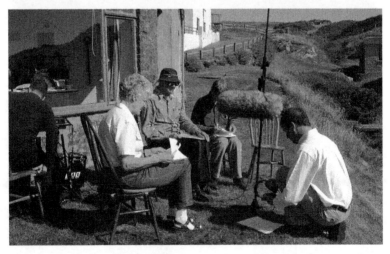

The Hookses; and final briefing for the *Sunday Worship* recording outside The Hermitage, broadcast in April 2004.

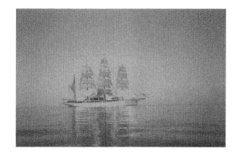 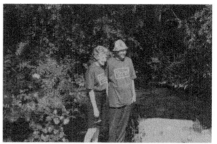

Sea Cloud, and joint winners of the Audubon award, 1992.

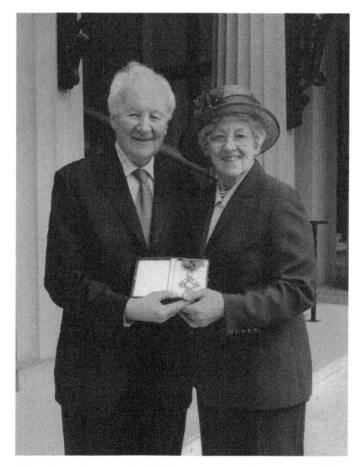

With John Stott at his CBE investiture at Buckingham Palace.

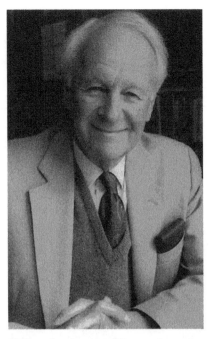

The photo of John that hung in Frances's study in Bourne End.

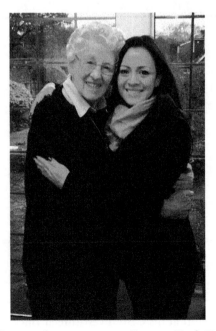

With Eidi Cruz in the sun room at Bourne End, December 2013.

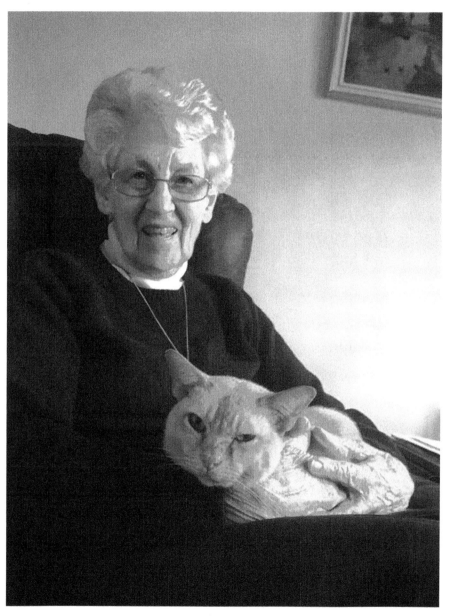

Frances, now in her nineties, with Ginger.

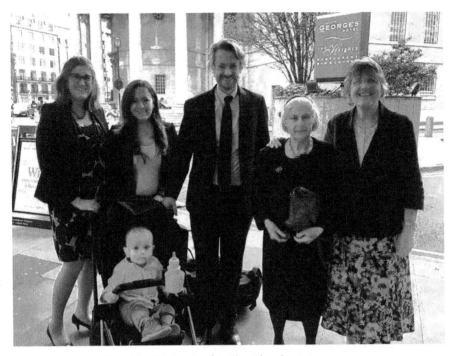

Outside All Souls after the Thanksgiving service.

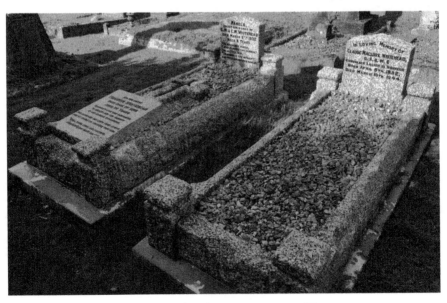

Whitehead family graves at Bovey Tracey.

CHAPTER SIXTEEN
From Bourne End to Bovey Tracey

Frances had never lost her affection for Bovey Tracey, her childhood home. Caroline Bowerman had taken her a book about the town and Frances would often find herself thinking of her childhood there. In her mind's eye, she would be back in Beara, in its fields behind the house, or at the blacksmiths with her pony. It was clear that her ashes should be buried in Bovey.

Amersham, 20 June 2019

The service for Frances's cremation took place in Amersham Crematorium, with just a few close friends present. Ben Homan, Director of Langham US, was staying with Chris and Liz Wright and they symbolically represented the global Langham movement, which had remained so close to Frances's heart from its very earliest beginnings as the Evangelical Literature Trust.

Viv Drake brought a collection of flowers from Frances's garden, including a cutting from the tree Frances had planted in memory of John, together with beautiful, long-stemmed pink tea roses, to share around Frances's friends. On entering the chapel, each of these roses was placed beside Frances's coffin as the familiar and confident aria from Handel could be heard: 'I know that my Redeemer liveth'. The service was led by Chris Wright.

Rose McIlrath recalled her fifty-year bond of friendship with Frances, how Frances had taught her as a young Christian, and given advice which was both spiritual and practical on many occasions. It had been a strong mutual friendship which had borne each of them through testing times. Viv Drake spoke of Frances as a neighbour and friend.

The service concluded with the Apostle Paul's firm words of affirmation from the *Messiah,* 'and the dead shall be raised incorruptible'. The choice of music echoed that which was playing in the sacred time in St Barnabas, as Frances and those with her stood around John Stott's bed as he died.

All Souls, 21 June 2019

The Thanksgiving service at All Souls was live-cast so friends around the world could be a part of it.[94] (See Appendix 4.) It opened with Wesley's declaratory hymn: 'Jesus! The Name high over all', sung as the Processional hymn at the memorial service for John Stott. For those who had been at that service in St Paul's Cathedral, with Frances in the front row, seated next to Jane Williams and awaiting the lead from the wandsman, there was an immediate link.

Old friends from All Souls days travelled considerable distances to be there. Neil and Jenny Woodward arrived from Australia in time for the cremation service the day before. Former Study Assistant John Yates III flew in from North Carolina, and Wendy Toulmin from the Congo. Toby Howarth, Bishop of Bradford and a former Study Assistant, travelled south from Yorkshire. Michael Nazir-Ali, former Bishop of Rochester and an early Langham scholar, read the scripture. Among others who came to express their gratitude for Frances were Bishop Graham Kings, now of Southwark Diocese and formerly on the All Souls staff, and George Verwer, founder of Operation Mobilization. Roy McCloughry, John Stott's first Study Assistant, and his wife, Helen, were in Italy at the time, so were watching the service on Roy's mobile phone, from a park bench in Verona. Nigel Padfield, a cousin of Frances once removed from the Whitley branch of the family[95] caught news of Frances's death by reading the obituary in *The Times* and came to All Souls. It was a very welcome surprise to have family, albeit distant family, at the service.

Frances had loved the music at All Souls, directed since 1972 by Dr Noel Tredinnick. Noel would retire from his role that month. There was a sense of completion in his drawing together an ensemble for the

Thanksgiving service for Frances, having directed the music for the funeral and the Thanksgiving service for John.

Mark Labberton, unable to be at the service, sent a tribute on video, describing Frances as the equivalent of 'a force field of five or more people' and recalling the way she shunted her caster-less chair across the carpet, and hauled out the drawers of the filing cabinet which were not on rollers. Her passion was in the service of Christ and she was a lioness in her protection of John's time. Heidi Cooper also brought smiles and laughter as she recalled her Bible studies with Frances, and how Frances had instinctively assumed the role of the teacher, asking Heidi to identify the 'dominant thought' of a passage; and testing her on learning scripture off by heart, not tolerating any lapses of memory. The current author reflected on Frances's unusual combination of gifts, her humility, her energy and her doggedness; and on God's providence in preparing Frances as a mathematician, so, as John Stott's global ministry grew, she could manage process, and think in categories, independent and inter-relating.

Matthew Smith read Frances's own account of her conversion to Christ; how she could 'barely find a seat in a side aisle' when she first heard John Stott preach in St Peter's Church a few months earlier; and how she was struck by both 'his manner and bearing', and 'the compelling seriousness' of the way he explained the Scriptures. Then she wrote: 'What I remember most of all that night [the night of 31 December 1952], as he was explaining the story of Nicodemus, was his repeated exhortation: "Don't look at me; look at Christ." So, for the first time in my life, it seemed to me that I consciously "looked at Jesus," saw him in all his beauty and grace, and prayed to him to be my Saviour.'[96] Matthew spoke of Frances's capacity for friendships with many people in which she gave more than she received; of her diligence; of the hundreds of days they had spent cooking together at The Hookses. For his family and his wife Eidi's family, friendship with Frances now extended to the third generation, as Frances had played with their little son, Joshy.

Chris Wright explained his choice of readings,[97] and focused in on Numbers 23:19, a verse Frances had learned by heart as a child, and had often returned to. God did not lie, and was faithful to his word;

it was to this word, through the ministries of All Souls, John Stott and Langham Partnership, that Frances had given her life. She had proved it to be a word which would always accomplish what is purposed. What might Frances's words of advice be to her friends, and those who cared for her? Firstly, to put their trust in Christ. And beyond that, to trust in the faithfulness of God; and to love, and live by, the word of God.

The congregation then rose for the closing hymn, Stuart Townend's and Keith Getty's great affirmation 'In Christ Alone, my hope is found'. Hugh Palmer invited a brief silence to gather thoughts and sadnesses, then spoke into them from Psalm 16:11. God will show us the path of life, and in his presence is fullness of joy.

In 2011 on the day of John Stott's funeral, Frances, and others close to John, had sat on the pavement outside Villandry's on Tottenham Court Road, to decompress after the emotional demands of his funeral service and cremation. Now it was the turn of those who had first talked in the sun room in Bourne End on Sunday 2 June to sit around a table, this time in the pizza restaurant next to All Souls, with Eidi and little Joshy. There were conversations after the service to be shared more widely; greetings to be extended; and plans to be set for the interment of ashes in Bovey Tracey.

Bovey Tracey, 1 July 2019

Graham Hamilton, vicar of the Church of St Peter, St Paul and St Thomas of Canterbury, opened the service with a welcome. While he had not met Frances, he had benefited from the fruit of her labour; and he was honoured for this service to be held in the church, known locally as 'PPT'. Mark Labberton, who had sent a video tribute for the Thanksgiving at All Souls, flew from California to lead the service.

Nigel Padfield and his brother, Richard, and their cousin Elizabeth, were there; as was Viv Styles, Manager of Bovey Heritage Centre.[98] The Bovey section of the *Mid Devon Advertiser* had given half a page to Frances's story that week, with a photograph of her in her Lambeth MA gown.[99]

As at All Souls, the service for the committal of ashes opened with Charles Wesley's hymn of praise to Jesus. Richard Padfield read from Philippians 2:1-11, taking opportunity first to tell of his Freshers' week at Newcastle University, in 1967. The Christian Union had a bookstall at the Freshers' Fair. As Richard glanced at the books, he noticed the title *Basic Christianity* by John Stott, and, knowing that Frances was working with Stott, decided to buy it.[100] The next day, he read it, and through its pages found faith in the risen Christ.[101]

Eidi Cruz-Valdivieso brought a perceptive and winsome tribute, based on her friendship with Frances for as long as she could remember. It is included in full as Appendix 1.

David Gallagher recalled the story of the extension to The Hermitage, following John Stott's eightieth birthday appeal; this showed the extent of responsibility Frances carried for The Hookses. To the mirth of those present, he related his journey with Frances to meet with the builders one Friday morning. They left London the evening before. David had failed to book accommodation in advance, and it proved almost impossible to find anywhere to stay. As they tried one place after another, it began to look likely that they would have to spend the night in the car. Frances, by now in her late seventies, regarded it as an exciting adventure, showing her capacity for spontaneity and her good humour.[102]

Mark Labberton spoke from two New Testament passages.[103]

It would be hard, he said, by human judgment, to find someone more deserving of Christ's commendation of the first servant in Matthew 25. Frances would no doubt underestimate the gifts she had been given, and surely undervalue the service she offered. But daily devotion was her centre of gravity.

Then he turned to the hymn in Philippians 2, which points supremely to Jesus. Here was the inspiration, he said, of Frances's sacrificial, other-centred life and love, which she so personally, genuinely, and whole-heartedly gave – to and alongside John Stott – for fifty-five years.

At the graveside, five minutes' walk away, in the town cemetery, Rose McIlrath and Mark Labberton together lowered the casket with

Frances's ashes into her sister Pamela's grave, lying alongside their father's grave. Mark wrote afterwards of this short time as being for him 'the most memorable, and unwitnessed, moment of that day.'

> 'Rose and I were next to one another on our knees, peering into the small opening of the grave. As we lowered Frances' urn into the ground, I couldn't but notice that though Rose's knees may have been older than mine, hers seemed the more nimble. Rose and I were holding strings looped into the handles on opposite ends of a basket that held the ashes. The uneven ground at the bottom of the grave made it difficult for two people to manipulate the basket so it would be completely flat on the ground. Without a word, Rose quickly seized the string from my hand, and, holding the remains of her beloved, lifelong friend, she delicately and determinedly made the small adjustment that levelled the basket just so – a final, fitting gesture of love. Well done, good and faithful servants.'

Once the ashes were lowered into the grave, Mark invited friends to share stories or words of appreciation before the final prayer. There was no sense of hurry. A flower arrangement of elegant long-stemmed roses had been brought from the church to the cemetery, and friends who wished to do so slowly moved forward, one by one, to place a rose in the grave.

In due course an angled plaque was laid on the grave, below Pamela's headstone, and mirroring its font. The inscriptions read:

PAMELA
Dearly loved child of
C M and E M WHITEHEAD
Died March 5th 1932
Aged 8 years.

The gardener asked,
'Who plucked this flower?'
The Master said,
'I plucked it for myself.'
And the gardener held his peace.

And her sister
FRANCES WHITEHEAD
Died June 1st 2019
Aged 94 years.

Frances's life was dedicated
To Christ and the growth
Of his church worldwide.
She assisted the Revd John Stott
For 55 years to further this end.

'Well done, good and faithful servant.' (Matthew 25:23)

This was truly the end of an era.

John and Frances served the purpose of God in their generation. It was one of the most exciting times in church history with massive growth, especially in China and in the Global South. As secular thinking took hold, big changes would soon be afoot in the church, and in the public arena.

We turn now to the ground they laid, under God, to strengthen and equip evangelicals.

AFTERWORD
A Shared Legacy

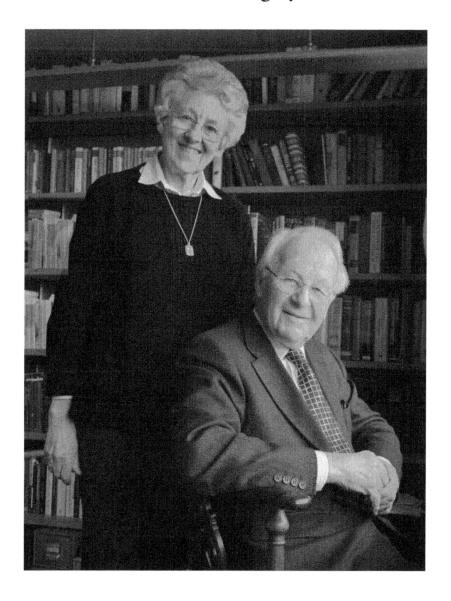

In 1999 John Stott became more conscious of his frailty. His older sister, Joanna, had died that year, leaving him as the only remaining member of his immediate family.

At Easter, Frances and John compiled a lengthy report, summarising John's continuing ministries, and the links each one had. Shortly afterwards, she typed a letter to Lindsay Brown, IFES General Secretary, whom John Stott had known since Lindsay's student days in Oxford in the 1970s. It was to ask if John could meet with Lindsay and a few of the senior staff at the IFES World Assembly, taking place in Seoul in July, to consider with him the future of these endeavours.

A critical decision

Addressing the Assembly at a special open meeting in the city's great Hallelujah Presbyterian Church, Uncle John said he sensed the need to pass the baton to a new generation of 'Timothys'. Here his thirty-seventh book, *Evangelical Truth,* was launched, carrying the subtitle 'A personal plea for truth and unity'. A few days later, on departure day, as the coaches filled up to take participants to the airport, the IFES senior leaders gathered for the meeting. Could the ministries John Stott had founded find a permanent home within the IFES structures? It soon became clear that there was much more to discuss than this exhausted group could properly manage. It was agreed to postpone the meeting.

The IFES leaders assembled again in November that year, in the UK, at the training centre for Wycliffe Bible Translators, not far from Heathrow airport. Here they were joined by John Stott, David Turner, Chris Wright, David Jones,[104] and leaders of each of the ministries. This meeting would be referred to by those involved as the 'Post-Stott Consultation'. Frances handled all the logistics, and ensured everyone had briefing papers. Among the IFES staff gathered were David Zac Niringyie (later Bishop of Kampala) who had founded the Kampala Institute of Christian Impact on the model of LICC;[105] Ziel Machado who had studied at LICC; and Las Newman from Jamaica. Las had first met Uncle John when he was aged twenty, and a first-year student at Ontario Bible College. In the spring term of that year, a week of mission was planned to the nearby University of Toronto, with Stott as the missioner. Las was asked to be his onsite personal assistant, and they had stayed in touch.

Lindsay Brown asked Las Newman (Caribbean), Ziel Machado (Latin America) and David Zac Niringiye (English- and Portuguese-speaking Africa) to speak of the impact of John's ministry in their regions. It had been profound for the whole of the IFES world. With converging goals in working to strengthen the Church in each nation, and with closely-aligned values, John Stott's idea of enveloping his ministries under IFES was not without merit. But what would work *most effectively* in terms of structure and capacity? Would the IFES mandate – with senior staff at full stretch – become overloaded and too diverse, if more were added? After unhurried discussion it was concluded that the better way forward was for IFES and John Stott's endeavours to remain separate, but closely connected.

The subsequent decision to appoint an International Director of what would become Langham Partnership was to prove the right way forward. Chris Wright had already been approached by John about the possibility of succeeding him in the leadership of the Langham programmes, but that was not yet known among others present. The meeting unanimously affirmed the nature and shape of the role Chris would take, while advocating an independent structure. Chris's own roots in IFES from his undergraduate days in Cambridge, and his personal friendships with several IFES Regional Secretaries, provided a smooth transition of leadership from John Stott, and the continuing strong links between the two movements.

In 2002 Las Newman was again hosting John Stott, this time in Jamaica, and accompanied by Chris Wright. Las had worked with Frances in handling the scheduling details, as was the typical pattern for all Stott's travels. Once more Las was asked to fulfil two of the same tasks he had undertaken for Uncle John in Toronto, thirty years earlier. He would schedule a time for John Stott to speak on the phone with the local Bishop; and, specifically asked by John himself, he would bring a selection of local view postcards, from which John could select one to send to Frances.

A shared six-fold legacy

Frances's role was crucial to each part of John Stott's legacy. Much of his influence was achieved through friendship. It was his trademark. There are many personal stories to be told of this. As Professor Nigel Cameron wrote to *The Times*, 'This gift of friendship, combined with his interdisciplinary and enquiring mind, equipped him to bring traditional Christianity to bear on science, medicine, contemporary thinking about war and nuclear deterrence and such big questions. He was perhaps uniquely able to convene that largely private discussion among the upper echelons of science and medicine and the armed forces... as he laboured mightily to bridge the Christian faith community and the hottest of emerging issues.' Speaking of 'his network of personal friendships which snaked across the face of the planet' Nigel Cameron, who had known John Stott since student days, concluded that 'friendship was embedded in his character, and was, more than anything else, the key to his astonishing influence.'[106]

Friendship is an art of which Stott was a master. And the art of building and maintaining these friendships never strayed far from Frances's desk. For they were anchored in arrangements for meetings – both in London and across the world; in letters by the thousands; in sending gifts of books; in handling prayer news as it came into the office; in arranging scholarships; in invitations to tea in Weymouth Street, or invitations to The Hookses. Letters, faxes and emails – all would receive a response typed by Frances – whether from student leaders; leaders in the public arenas; leaders in the church; leaders in mission agencies; or from boys like Saúl Cruz – enquiries sent initially to Dr Stott, John or Uncle John would continue with questions to Miss Whitehead, soon addressed as Frances or Auntie Frances.

As we look at each part of the Stott legacy, we can trace its beginning back to a friendship. For it was through friendships, facilitated by Frances in a thousand ways, that confidence was won, ideas were shared, and new projects ventured. Here we will look at the major arenas of influence. Our purpose is simply to give an overview, and dip deeper in just a few areas.

Books: John Stott wrote some fifty books, published in English and in translation;

Langham Partnership: A three-fold ministry to strengthen the church in the Majority World, through the provision of books, scholarships, and training in preaching;

Lausanne Movement, the global movement founded by Billy Graham for more strategic efforts in world evangelization: in the geographical world, and in the world of ideas;

London Institute for Contemporary Christianity (LICC), helping Christians to bring the presence of Christ into the workplace and the public arena;

International Fellowship of Evangelical Students (IFES), growing from movements in ten nations to one hundred and fifty nations in John Stott's lifetime;

New Anglican endeavours: (i) the Evangelical Fellowship in the Anglican Communion (EFAC), and (ii) its English and Welsh affiliates: the Church of England Evangelical Council (CEEC) and the Evangelical Fellowship in the Church in Wales (EFCW); and (iii) the National Evangelical Anglican Congress (NEAC).

1. Books

John Stott's writing formed a distinct corpus of work which would need to be looked after with care. His lucid exposition and his desire to engage critical issues have become a lasting gift to the church, now in many languages. The *Bible Speaks Today* series, Stott's idea, and of which he was New Testament Editor – broke new ground in combining exposition and application for laymen and pastors alike. To oversee the future of Stott's writing, a small group of Literary Executors was set up in 1996.[107] Frances was appointed an Executor in her own right from the outset, and continued in that role until 2011, remaining a consultant to the group.

In characteristic fashion, John Stott was the first Chair of the Literary Executors, then passed the role the following year to his friend and publisher, Frank Entwistle of IVP. [108] He knew his books would percolate though each strand of his legacy, and he remained active as a Literary Executor for as long as he was able. (The meetings moved down to St Barnabas after 2007, so he could participate.) We see more of his influence through books when we look at Langham Partnership.

2. Langham Partnership

Chris Wright was appointed International Ministries Director of the newly-formed Langham Partnership in 2001. Under Chris, John Stott's 'Abrahamic and Apostolic' ministry, as outlined below, would be taken forward with careful strategy and a driven passion.[109]

This tri-fold ministry had begun with the Evangelical Literature Trust (ELT), founded in 1971. From then, all royalties from Stott's books, amounting to hundreds of thousands of pounds, would, in his word, be 'recycled', that is, used for the provision of books for pastors and seminary libraries in the Majority World. Frances administered the Trust for its first six years. An early priority was to handle discussions with the Inland Revenue to ensure that no tax should to be paid on these earnings.

Langham Literature

In 1977 Frances was able to hand over the administration of the ELT to Ronald Inchley, founding Publisher of Inter-Varsity Press, on his retirement. RI, as he was always known, had encouraged John Stott as a young writer, as he had also encouraged the young Jim Packer, Michael Green, Michael Griffiths, and others who had grown up in the British university Christian Unions.[110]

RI's taking over the ELT from Frances was a model oft-replicated. As we have seen, John Stott would come up with an idea, discuss it with Frances or later with the happy triumvirate, then with a few friends in ministries in the area to which it pertained. With Frances's help, he would get it off the ground, then, when the right person for the job came in view, the responsibility would, in Frances's words, be 'flipped onto that person's shoulders'.

In 1983 the ELT leadership was passed to John Hayden, a vicar in East Anglia.[111] Over the years, library grants, for purchasing books at specially-negotiated discounts, would go to a thousand seminary libraries in the Majority World. Further, John Stott's own books, originally typed by Frances at The Hookses, and translated into around sixty languages, would help some 35,000 pastors to build a personal library; in addition 10,000 graduates would receive two higher-level books each year.

Within twenty years of founding the ELT, Stott's ministry reached into over a hundred countries in the Majority World, providing books of substance for pastors and scholars, in major languages and in local languages.

In 2001, when Langham Partnership was formed, the Evangelical Literature Trust merged with the Langham Trust and was re-named 'Langham Literature', under the leadership of Pieter Kwant. By the time of John Stott's death, some twenty-five thousand books were being supplied annually to pastors and scholars, and a further fifteen thousand to Bible College and seminary libraries in more than seventy-five countries.[112]

Langham Scholars

Frances administered the Langham Scholars programme for its first fifteen years. As John Stott explained: 'Our vision should be to help capture the seminaries of the world for the gospel. To do this, we have to ensure (as far as we can) that the world's seminaries are staffed by scholar-saints – that is, by men and women who combine in themselves academic excellence and personal godliness.'

To 'help capture the seminaries' John Stott and others would work to identify some of the most able theological thinkers in the Majority World, and provide scholarships so they could gain a doctorate or pursue post-doctoral research in the West, then return to their own country to teach in a seminary or university.

Frances worked out the allowance each scholar would need, looking at family circumstances and their place of study, and administered each of their accounts. They would largely come to UK universities with conservative faculty under whom they could study: often

Oxford or Cambridge, Birmingham, Manchester, Edinburgh or Aberdeen. In some cases they would go to the US, which may require a higher bursary. Frances was a member in her own right of the Langham Trust Scholarship Committee, which carried responsibility for selecting candidates.

Now more than three hundred Langham scholars are serving the global church in a range of positions – in church leadership, in seminaries and in the public arenas. Each year, a further dozen or more complete doctorates, and new scholarships are awarded. In tune with the spirit of John Stott's passion for devolving leadership, and the growth of the evangelical church in the Majority World, the Langham Scholar programme was from 2012 led by Revd Dr Riad Kassis, himself an Arab Langham Scholar, based in his home country of Lebanon.[113]

Langham Preaching

The third arrow in the Langham quiver is Langham Preaching, which embodies the heartbeat of Langham's vision. Its purpose is to strengthen the handling of scripture, so churches will grow to maturity, and be equipped for their mission in the world.

Careful Bible exposition had been a value close to Stott's own heart from his student days. He had, metaphorically, sat at the feet of Charles Simeon, and imbibed much from the models given him in the CICCU. Stott himself was later to be the one setting the model, and his *I Believe in Preaching* became regarded as a classic work. Now, through his endeavour, with Frances's support, a global movement to strengthen preaching would be established. This began when John Stott and Chris Wright were invited to conduct seminars for preachers in Peru and Argentina in October 2001. It was launched as a full programme of Langham Partnership in 2002 under the pioneering leadership of Jonathan Lamb.[114]

By the time John Stott died, Langham Preaching was training and supporting thousands of pastors and lay preachers in some 50 countries, through national networks, with indigenous leaders running training events and local preachers' clubs. After a decade of growth under Jonathan Lamb, which was a source of great joy to both John and Frances, the leadership transferred to Paul Windsor, a New Zealander living in India.

3. Lausanne Movement

Both John and Frances expended much energy over the course of two decades on the work of the Lausanne Movement, which now has a presence in 198 nations. Its purpose and essence remains as it was from the outset, namely to draw evangelicals to work together 'to bring the whole gospel to the whole world'. That is the geographical world, and the world of ideas.

John Stott was chief architect of *The Lausanne Covenant* (1974) and *The Manila Manifesto* (1989) which issued from its first two global gatherings. Both John and Frances had been onsite in Pattaya (1980); and with help from Frances, John had edited the Movement's major consultation papers (1990s).

Lausanne, as the Movement is widely known, went through its 'quiet years' in the 1990s; then, under new leadership by Doug Birdsall from the US, and Lindsay Brown, former IFES General Secretary, it was awakened and re-energised. Chris Wright was drawn in to chair its Theology Working Group, for which John Stott had been the first chair. Blair Carlson, who for twenty years set up Billy Graham's crusades around the world, adopting much the same format as that of Harringay, directed the Third Lausanne Congress, held in Cape Town in 2010.

Following in the role John Stott had taken in Lausanne and Manila, Chris Wright was chair of the Statement Working Group in Cape Town and chief architect of the two-part the *Cape Town Commitment*.[115] In March 2011, as soon as the *Commitment* was published, a copy was sent straight to Frances in Weymouth Street. She took it down to St Barnabas that week and began to read it aloud to John. A few days later, Doug Birdsall received his copy at his home in Boston, and called John Stott straight away. Phillip Herbert, a regular visitor and one of John's most faithful friends, answered the phone. Phillip was, at the time, continuing to read it out, section by section, from where

Frances had left off. 'You seem to have achieved an astonishing degree of unity,' Stott said to Doug, when Phillip handed him the phone.

Each of the ministries and endeavours with which John Stott had been closely associated over the course of his ministry was part of the Third Lausanne Congress. All the matters in which he had yearned for evangelicals to engage were laid out here – not just in a document, but in a *commitment*, in response to God's covenantal love. He knew of the unhurried process before and during the Congress, to listen to voices of evangelical leaders from across the world; to discern what the Holy Spirit is saying to the church. Further, John Stott had heard of plans being laid for global consultations to take forward the major areas in the *Commitment*. No doubt there was a sense of completion as he listened to the *Cape Town Commitment* being read to him, while sensing he would soon be with Christ.

4. London Institute for Contemporary Christianity (LICC)

While John Stott was travelling widely, the London Institute drew many younger staff from IFES member movements, and young professionals with whom he had talked. We have read some of their stories. Its focus now may be summed up as twofold: empowering lay people to be fruitful for Christ out on their daily 'frontlines': at work, in meetings, in the community etc; and envisioning and enabling local churches to disciple them to do so. For, as Mark Greene, Director since 1999, said at the Memorial Service in St Paul's Cathedral, John Stott 'yearned not only for the conversion of medics, lawyers, and factory workers, he yearned for the transformation of medicine, law and manufacturing.'

In the early 1980s Stott coined the phrase 'double listening', urging that Christians listen to God through scripture, and listen to the world. While the voices are not given equal weight, both must be heard and understood if Truth is to be applied in the workplace and the public square. Through courses, lectures and publications, the London Institute provides training for Christians in this double listening, so they can shake salt and shine light more effectively.

The London Lectures, founded in 1974 and from 2013 renamed the John Stott London Lectures, provide a further means of understanding societal trends, and helping Christians to think more deeply about major issues. Their goal is to expound an aspect of historical biblical Christianity and relate it to a contemporary issue; and to do so at a scholarly level, presented in a way which engages educated laymen. Through publishing and online distribution, their benefits reach many more than the physical audience.

5. International Fellowship of Evangelical Students (IFES)

Frances scheduled John Stott's overseas trips, and these would always include aspects of IFES ministry: meetings with staff, and often student events at which he had been invited to speak.

Frances and Rose were both at the opening of the new offices in Oxford for IFES and its British movement, UCCF.[116] The rooms in the new building had been named after events or places, or people who, under God, had helped to shape their story.[117] On the ground floor hangs a framed engraving of Charles Simeon, similar to the one which hung on John Stott's wall. On the top floor is 'Uncle John's Library'.

John Stott conducted university missions to over forty of the world's universities, and spoke at meetings in many more. He understood the strategic nature of the university as few do, and would gather groups of specialists in different fields, together with the most promising young graduates he had met in those fields, to help forge a Christian mind in that area. He chose Inter-Varsity Press as his primary publisher, always encouraging students to read more and to think deeply.

Following his fall in 2006, he was unable to join the IFES World Assembly in the summer of 2007, in Canada. With help from Frances, and from Kharis Productions, he sent a greeting by video, recorded at The Hookses. He said: 'I would like to introduce myself to you as a committed 'IFES man' – and that for at least four reasons. IFES is (i) biblical, seeking in all things to be submissive to the supreme authority of scripture; (ii) indigenous, encouraging self-governing national movements; (iii) evangelistic, with students winning students for Christ; and (iv) holistic, seeking to lead new converts to maturity in Christ. So I thank God for IFES.' The hall of staff and students spontaneously rose to their feet and applauded.

John Stott was a friend and advisor to generations of staff and students in IFES and its national movements. Where he saw gifts to be further developed, he opened the way for scholarships, to LICC or for further academic study in universities. His genuine friendships led him to make connections and introductions, and to follow stories as people moved into ministry or the professions.[118] He, as an Anglican, and Martyn Lloyd-Jones, as a Free Churchman, publicly anchored the movement in the church, adding their endorsement of its doctrinal and intellectual credibility.

6. New Anglican endeavours (EFAC, CEEC, EFCW, NEAC)

We have seen the way Stott's new ideas would be shared first with Frances, and from 1978 with his Study Assistant, then with a few others; and how Frances would carry the management side until it could be passed to someone else. Forty years before the term 'Fresh Expressions' was used in evangelism, John Stott founded the All Souls Clubhouse in the poorer part of his parish. The meeting of Ministers in University Towns, begun by John Stott with his friends Douglas Johnson and Oliver Barclay, formed a fellowship which worked and prayed to see an evangelical church within reach of every university; the All Souls International Fellowship became a model for wider work among international students. We could go on . . .

Stott described himself not as an 'evangelical Anglican', but as an 'Anglican evangelical' – with 'evangelical' as the noun. While his denomination was secondary to his biblical faith, his Anglican roots and rooting were always clear. Two initiatives to which John Stott and Frances Whitehead gave much time were the Evangelical Fellowship in the Anglican Communion (EFAC) and one of its founding members, the Church of England Evangelical Council (CEEC).

In 1960, CEEC was launched to unite and provide a forum for Anglican evangelicals. By 1961, the wider EFAC had been formed, with member movements in two Australian states, in New Zealand

and in Tanganyika, under the leadership of the Archbishop of Sydney and Primate of Australia, with John Stott and Bishop Marcus Loane as co-secretaries. By the following year it had taken off globally, with *The Churchman*, an academic and respected evangelical publication as its news organ.[119] The 39 Articles of the Church of England formed its doctrinal basis. While stronger at some times than at others, the EFAC networks have proved of clear worth over the decades as the Church has been assailed by liberal scholarship and *mores*. In recent years, the Church Society, the Global Anglican Future Congress (GAFCON) and Anglican Mainstream have assumed significant profiles as rallying calls for orthodoxy. EFAC created the basis for this in the early 1960s.

Evangelicals were very few in the Church in Wales, and John Stott would invite them to The Hookses once a year for fellowship. These 'Dale Days' were a source of encouragement and affirmation. In March 1967 the Evangelical Fellowship in the Church in Wales (EFCW) was formed.

Later that year the CEEC would gather for the first National Evangelical Anglican Congress (NEAC), at the University of Keele. John Stott was to play an active role in the first two Congresses, and to lead the listening group in NEAC3, as outlined in Chapter 8. Frances accompanied John to NEAC4 in the Blackpool Winter Gardens in 2003, where they were given seats which overlooked the main hall. Their role was now to urge others on.

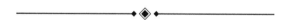

John Stott and Frances Whitehead lent support to several overseas ventures. We have traced the role played by Frances from receiving a letter written by the young Saúl Cruz, to his establishing Armonia amid the poverty of Jalalpa in Mexico City. One final vignette – from South Asia.

A refuge for women in Tamil Nadu

On a visit to the state of Tamil Nadu in South India, in 1994, John Stott met Mercy Abraham, a young woman who had founded a refuge in her own home for abused women. She was accused locally of running a brothel; in addition her Hindu father had not spoken to her for four years as she had refused to marry her cousin. Stott was moved by her story, and her steadfast Christian testimony. 'I am the same age as your father,' he said, when he had coaxed her to tell him about her situation. Perhaps remembering his estrangement from his own father,[120] he then added – as reported in Mercy's words several years later – 'From now on, think of me as your father.' Seeing her resolute stance for Christ and her compassion for local women, he undertook to help her financially, and urged her to look for some land where she could build a refuge.

In 2000, by now married to Vinci from Switzerland,[121] Mercy reported:

> We found a suitable plot of land 15k from Dharmapuri. When I got in touch with Uncle John he sent ten times what he had promised, with only one request – to plant lots of fruit trees so that the birds would come there . . . Because of his help we were able to purchase seven acres, dig a well, build a small watchman's house and plant 1500 fruit trees! The birds have come in their hundreds, as well as hundreds of women and children who have a safe and beautiful place to find peace and physical, emotional and spiritual help.

In 2001, John invited Mercy and Vinci over to London, with their little girl, Persis, and he and Frances planned an itinerary which included meetings with Tearfund, some sightseeing, and worship at All Souls. Further, Frances sent invitations to a group of John's friends in All Souls who had financial means, to meet Mercy and hear of her work. Hers was a project which would give rich spiritual returns for their financial investment. Gifts that week enabled the purchase of a further fifteen acres of land.

By 2012, the Mahalir Aran ('Refuge for women') Trust owned a forty-acre site with a farm, and cared for ninety residents in three hostels, providing a safe refuge, and the chance to learn new skills. In that Hindu region, where 'it is difficult to find one Christian in ten thousand', Mercy Abraham was now planning to build a church.

'We plan to call it the Eastgate Church,' she said, 'and we will use the same discipleship model that Jesus used of equipping local pastors and sending them out.'[122]

The land Mercy and Vinci had purchased proved to be a fine source of granite. The church building in Mercy's prayerful imagining would be round. She wrote from her experience of England: 'The style would be traditional Anglican, modelled in the Round Church style of Cambridge, and All Souls Langham Place.' It would, she added, 'be dedicated to the glory of God, in memory of John Stott; and the quarried land will be levelled to plant more fruit trees, including mangoes, guavas and cashew nuts.' Few would have had a better feel for the demands of the fruit harvesting than Frances, from her long-ago Beara days, and her mother's fruit farm in South Africa. Frances kept an active interest in plans for the Eastgate Church for as long as she was able. David Gallagher had designed it. The son of missionary parents, he had grown up in India, which added a poetic touch to the story. David would continue to work closely with Mercy and Vinci on plans to expand the ministry. Theirs, as so many of the endeavours in which Frances played a role, remain unfinished stories.

Armonia and the Mahalir Aran Trust are not only supported financially and in prayer by All Souls, but the church sends students and young graduates each year to Mexico and to Tamil Nadu, on Wetfoot Teams, to 'get their feet wet' in cross-cultural mission. So the friendships begun by John and Frances are being passed down to a new generation. And the manifold legacy of Weymouth Street, in which John Stott planted and first Frances, and then many others, watered, sees God continuing to give growth.

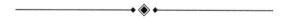

All Souls Church, Langham Place, where Frances found faith in Christ, is unlikely ever to be separated in people's minds from John Stott's name. The church had an evangelical heritage before he joined its staff; indeed it was when Harold Earnshaw-Smith, then Rector, was speaking at a CICCU meeting in 1945, that he asked Stott if he would consider a curacy there. No-one could have imagined his appointment as Rector less than five years later.

It was under John Stott's leadership of All Souls, with Frances Whitehead as Church Secretary, that new ideas for parish ministry were formed – the All Souls Clubhouse, Bible Schools, Commissioned Workers, All Souls International Fellowship. Each is a story in itself. In the mid 1970s, the Waldegrave Hall was constructed beneath All Souls, a legacy of Michael Baughen's leadership. This created significant new capacity for the church. The staff team began to expand in Michael Baughen's years, and has extended further under the leadership of Richard Bewes and Hugh Palmer.

At the invitation of each of his three succeeding Rectors, John Stott remained as Rector Emeritus of All Souls, holding the title until he died. It was as Rector Emeritus that a seat was reserved for him on the left side of the platform, where he would be seen every Sunday when at home in London. Until 2006 he remained on the preaching team. John and Frances became a familiar sight, walking up Portland Place after the Sunday evening service, and as John got frailer in later years, they walked arm in arm.

John Stott's flat in Bridford Mews is now used as accommodation for All Souls staff. The cook's bedroom on the ground floor of 12 Weymouth Street, which became Frances's office for over forty years, is, fittingly, used by the All Souls minister for world mission.

Until 2012 Frances continued to drive up to town from Bourne End on a Sunday afternoon, for the All Souls evening service. Her membership of the church family stretched back for almost six decades.

———————— ◆ ————————

A story to be preserved

And so it was Frances Whitehead who gave the opening tribute in the Memorial Service for John Stott in St Paul's Cathedral. For as we have seen, the 'Archangel in charge of postings', to borrow again from the letter Stott received from a friend in 1956, had not only kept John in London, but had, in addition, kept Frances alongside him.

It was a particular calling – a shared calling – of two particular people for a particular time in church history; a partnership and a growing friendship which would remain focused on that calling, not without cost; an unrelenting pace for over half a century. This, then, is the back-story to John Stott's colossal influence; a story unlikely to be re-enacted, and needing to be preserved.

APPENDICES

APPENDIX 1
Tributes to Frances Whitehead

Tributes from the thanksgiving service at All Souls, and the service for the interment of ashes at Bovey Tracey, are available in full at *dictumpress.com*. They bring out different facets of Frances's nature and her character.

Below is the tribute from Eidi Cruz-Valdivieso, wife of Matthew Smith. It was given at the committal service in Bovey Tracey, and describes a unique friendship across generations and continents. This friendship originated in Frances's letter to Eidi's father (p120), when he was barely a teenager.

> It was 2007, and Uncle John Stott was moving imminently to the College of St Barnabas. One evening, after the service at All Souls, Matthew and I went downstairs to meet Frances like we would do every Sunday during those days. Frances received us with a big smile and showed us a little model that she had built to the exact scale of the studio where Uncle John would now live at the College. She wanted to know which furniture they could take, what it would look like in the different possible configurations and make sure that everything would be located in the right place. I had been impressed many times by Frances, but I think the minute little desk and bookshelves that Frances had perfectly built for this model ignited a whole new level of admiration for her work.
>
> Frances showed her love for God's work in everything she did and indeed in the friendships that she built. Her devotion to Uncle John and his ministry was joyful, and her sense of excellence came so naturally to her and was obvious to all. I had known

Frances for many years, and had known of her for as long as I could remember. Seeing Frances in action was indeed impressive: working in her office in the earlier years, when I used to visit from Mexico; or having one of the many conversations about my future or my studies; or when once, at The Hookses, she didn't even blink when I accidentally dropped her freshly-made cheesecake on the floor. Instead, she giggled with me until she made me feel comfortable again and could forget the incident.

Frances and I became very close during the time I lived in London and, in God's grace, shared significant moments after that. Spending time with Uncle John and with Frances during those years was such a privilege, an enormous blessing, one of my little-girl dreams. For as long as I can remember, the story of my Dad becoming a Christian through Uncle John's book, *Basic Christianity*, at the age of thirteen, and then writing to Uncle John to ask questions about his new faith, and then receiving a letter from his secretary, Frances Whitehead, was one of the most treasured stories in our family. In her letter, Frances apologised for not speaking Spanish and mentioned that Uncle John would be in Mexico City the following year and suggested my Dad could meet him there. A lifelong story started then.

In God's plan, it was through that letter, one of the thousands of letters that Frances lovingly and diligently replied to, that I'm here today giving thanks to God for her life, for her ministry and for her friendship. When my parents decided to sell everything and work with the poorest of the poor in Mexico City, Uncle John and Frances were such a loving source of prayerful encouragement. For many around the world, their influence was not only because of Uncle John's writing, preaching and teaching, but also because of the way he and Frances lived their lives, a simple lifestyle with the most remarkable amount of productivity that spoke so clearly about Christian integrity and vision. I come from Mexico and can testify to the depth of influence that Uncle John's and Frances's work had globally, and to the importance that their legacy has for my generation, and should have for the new generations of youth and children who need examples and teachers like them.

During the last few weeks, when going through the tears that we shed when a friend departs, I have reflected on how amazing it has been that although Frances was over fifty years my senior, God allowed me to have her as a close friend. Our different cultures, our different contexts and our different life seasons brought a sense of joy to our relationship rather than lack of understanding. Even more, and I believe I say this for generations of women and men around the world, Frances' example of Christian discipleship is of much learning and inspiration for many, and it certainly is for me. Her influence came, as it did with Uncle John, not only from their brilliance but through such a clear sense of integrity: their seeking of justice, their loving compassion and their walking humbly with our Lord. Indeed, as has been mentioned during these last few days, their ministry and partnership were one of a kind in history.

When reading Frances's biography, and imagining all that Frances's life was, we have nothing but gratitude to God for his love, and for the richness of the life he wants us to have in him – and with others, and in community – as we work for his Kingdom.

So I say goodbye, for now, my dear Frances. I thank God profoundly for your life, for the ministry he gave you, for the moments we shared, and for allowing me to be your friend.

APPENDIX 2 (I)

Books typed by Frances Whitehead

We show the date of first publication only. Several titles were taken over by other publishers for later editions. Almost all are still in print, some having changed their title to cross the Atlantic, or to fit better into a new publisher's list.

A. Books by John Stott

Basic Christianity (IVP, 1958)

Your Confirmation (Hodder, 1958)

What Christ thinks of the Church: Expository addresses on the first three chapters of the Book of Revelation (Lutterworth, 1958)

The Preacher's Portrait: Some New Testament word studies (Tyndale, 1961)

The Epistles of John: An Introduction and Commentary (Tyndale, 1964)

The Baptism and Fullness of the Holy Spirit (IVF, 1964)

The Canticles and Selected Psalms (Hodder, 1966)

Men Made New: An exposition of Romans 5-8 (IVP-UK; IVP-US, both 1966)

Our Guilty Silence: The Church, the Gospel and the World (EFAC with Hodder 1967)

One People: Clergy and Laity in God's Church (Falcon, 1969)

Christ the Controversialist: A study in some essentials of evangelical religion (Tyndale; IVP-UK, both 1970)

Understanding the Bible (Scripture Union and Gospel Light, 1972)

Your Mind Matters: The place of the mind in the Christian life (IVP-UK; IVP-US, both 1972)

Balanced Christianity: A call to avoid unnecessary polarisation (Hodder/IVP, 1975)

Christian Mission in the Modern World (Falcon/IVP, 1975)

The Lausanne Covenant: An exposition and Commentary (Worldwide Publications, USA 1975) also published as *Explaining the Lausanne Covenant* (Scripture Union, UK, 1975)

Focus on Christ: An enquiry into the Theology of Presuppositions (Collins UK and USA, both 1979)

The Bible: Book for Today (IVP-UK and IVP-US, both 1982)

I Believe in Preaching (Hodder and Eerdmans, both 1982). US title: *Between Two Worlds: The art of Preaching in the Twentieth Century*

Issues Facing Christians Today (Marshalls, 1984)

The Authentic Jesus: A response to current scepticism in the Church (Marshalls and IVP-US, both 1985)

The Whole Christian (IVP Korea, 1986)

The Cross of Christ (IVP-UK and IVP-US, both 1986)

Essentials: A liberal-evangelical dialogue (co-author David L. Edwards. Hodder, 1988)

The Lordship of Christ in South Africa (Lectures given in major cities; published by African Enterprise, Pietermaritzburg. Some lectures formed part of the text in *The Contemporary Christian*)

The Contemporary Christian: An urgent plea for double listening (IVP-UK and IVP-US, both 1992)

Problems of Christian Leadership (translated into Spanish as *Desafíos del liderazgo*. Certeza Argentina, Buenos Aires, 1992 and as *Los Problemas del Liderazgo Cristiano*, Ediciones PUMA, Lima / AGUEP, Lima, 1994)

People called to be Different (Translated into Spanish, *Llamados a ser diferentes*. IINDEF, Costa Rica, 1998)

Evangelical Truth: A personal plea for unity (IVP-UK and IVP-US, both 1999). In US subtitled: *A personal plea for Unity, Integrity and Faithfulness.*

The Birds our Teachers: Biblical lessons from a lifelong birdwatcher (Also subtitled *Essays in Orni-theology*) (Candle Books, 1999)

The Incomparable Christ: Based on the AD 2000 London Lectures in Contemporary Christianity (IVP-UK and IVP-US, both 2001)

Calling Christian Leaders: Biblical models of church, gospel and ministry (IVP-UK 2002) and with subtitle: *Basic Christian leadership* (IVP-US, also 2002)

People my Teachers: Around the world in eighty years (Candle Books, 2002)

The Church in the New Millennium: Three studies in the Acts of the Apostles (Zapf Chancery, Eldoret, Kenya, 2002)

Why I am a Christian: This is my story (IVP-UK and IVP-US, both 2003)

Through the Bible Through the Year: Daily reflections from Genesis to Revelation (Candle Books, UK and Baker Books, USA, both 2006)

The Living Church: Convictions of a Lifelong Pastor (IVP-UK and IVP-US, both 2007)

The Last Word: Reflections on a Lifetime of Preaching. Keswick address, 2007. (Keswick Classics, Authentic Media UK, US and India, all 2008)

John Stott at Keswick: A lifetime of preaching. Keswick addresses. (Keswick Classics, Authentic Media UK, US and India, all 2008)

The Radical Disciple: Wholehearted Christian Living (IVP-UK; IVP-US, both 2010). In US subtitled: *Some Neglected aspects of our Calling.*

Students of the Word: Engaging with Scripture to impact our world. Addresses given to IFES Graduates Conference, 2006. (IFES, 2013)

The Bible Speaks Today series (All Inter Varsity Press, UK and USA)

The Message of Galatians (1968) Subtitled *Only One Way*

The Message of 2 Timothy (1973) Subtitled *Guard the Gospel*

The Message of the Sermon on the Mount (1978) Subtitled *Christian Counter-Culture*

The Message of Ephesians (1979) Subtitled *God's New Society*

The Message of Acts (UK 1990) Subtitled *To the Ends of the Earth;* Published in US as *The Spirit, the Church and the World* (1990)

The Message of Thessalonians (1991) Subtitled *Preparing for the Coming King.* Published in US as *The Gospel and the End of Time* (1991)

The Message of Romans (UK, 1994) Subtitled *God's Good News for the World.* Published in US as *Romans: God's Good News for the World* (also 1994)

The Message of 1 Timothy and Titus (UK, 1996). Subtitled *The Life of the Local Church.* Published in US as *Guard the Truth* (also 1996)

B. Books by Timothy Dudley-Smith

Authentic Christianity: From the writings of John Stott, chosen and introduced by Timothy Dudley-Smith (IVP-UK, 1995; IVP-US, 1996)

John Stott: A comprehensive bibliography (IVP-UK, 1995; IVP-US, 1996)

John Stott: The Making of a Leader (Authorized biography Vol 1, IVP-UK and IVP-US, both 1999)

John Stott: A Global Ministry (Authorized biography Vol 2, IVP-UK and IVP-US, both 2001)

APPENDIX 2 (II)

The story of a biography

The original idea for an authorized biography of John Stott came from Richard Bewes in 1991 when Timothy Dudley-Smith, then Bishop of Thetford, a friend of John's since Cambridge days and a gifted writer, well-known for his hymnody, was approaching retirement. It was realized that unofficial biographies would soon begin to appear, so an official one would keep the record straight. This biography was eventually published in two volumes, in 1999 and 2001.[123] As the biography was being researched, it spawned along the way a new composite title of John Stott's work, *Authentic Christianity*, and a complete bibliography of his writing.

Frances Whitehead typed both volumes of the biography. A few years after the second volume was published, Bishop Timothy's older daughter, Caroline Gill, wrote to Frances to invite her to contribute to a biographical album, to be presented to Caroline's father on his eightieth birthday. The particular invitation was to write about her work on the *John Stott* biography. Given its seminal nature, and the adventure-ful story of its preparation for print, I offer Frances Whitehead's amusing account in full.

13 December 2005

Dear Caroline

The request to write a contribution to the Birthday Memento for Timothy Dudley-Smith went round and round in my head for many days – how could I begin to write about his massive two-volume Biography of John Stott in a way which would be worthy of the author and his subject? So I began by taking the

239

two volumes off the shelf and looking at them afresh, only to be struck once more by the vast amount of work which had gone into Timothy's MS, covering in twenty-eight chapters the eight decades of John Stott's life and times, from 1921-2000.

Here are some statistics: I went into the kitchen and weighed the two volumes in at 4lbs 6oz! Then I started counting: the main text covers approximately 1,000 pages, probably amounting to about 450,000 words (although this is after TDS had had to reduce the first draft typescript considerably); further pages cover 2,500 footnotes and about 600 bibliographic entries! What a work, what an author, what dedication, what thoroughness lie behind these figures. And all this was undertaken after Bishop Timothy had started his so-called 'retirement'! He began in 1991, at the instigation of Richard Bewes, and it took him ten years to complete, Volume I being published in 1999 and Volume 2 in 2001. How did he do it?

Well, he did not have the benefit of much modern technology at his finger tips – he did have a typewriter of some kind, and of course a fountain pen (no biro for this author!), red ink as well as blue, scissors, a ruler, sellotape and glue, and reams of paper! And he had a tape recorder for the many interviews he had with friends of JRWS who were willing to reminisce.

So after much background reading, correspondence and interviews, he began to write his MS and send it to me for typing, chapter by chapter at a time. I well remember how each batch would arrive at 12 Weymouth Street in a large, strong envelope, amply reinforced with sellotape on any suspect seam, and clearly addressed to me in his distinctive handwriting. I would set the chapter aside for some convenient day when JRWS might be abroad and I would have a bit more time to concentrate on the careful instructions which always accompanied each chapter to make sure I could follow the sequence of events! For the pages consisted of a mixture of typed and handwritten text, sometimes written between lines ruled carefully across the page to indicate a footnote, and all this interspersed with numerous photocopied extracts from some relevant document which had been carefully cut up and pasted onto the page. In addition there were always asterisks and arrows in appropriate places to help the typist along the way!

After the first typing came the author's corrections and deletions to bring the MS down to manageable length, but for me this was not such a huge task. But for TDS I can have nothing but the greatest admiration for the amazing way in which he brought this splendid biography to birth – and as JRWS frequently comments, he has been fortunate to have TDS as his biographer, with his 'meticulous research' and 'felicitous prose'. To which I say 'Amen'.

All best wishes as you put everything together.

Frances

[A few days later Caroline responded with the family's warmest thanks for such a 'MARVELLOUS contribution'.]

Within a short time of John Stott's death, less-careful writing, as surmised, began to appear. All future historians will be grateful for Timothy Dudley-Smith's 'meticulous research and felicitous prose', anchored in his knowledge of his subject, and of the times. Typing the manuscript was in itself a Herculean task, as we may infer from this piece; and no small feat for Frances to fit it into an already-full schedule. No doubt her own desire for accurate accounts to be published spurred her on. With a gift from Bishop Timothy to express his appreciation of her labour of love, she purchased a green Ekones chair and footstool, which she used every day in her sun room in Bourne End.

APPENDIX 3

Staff appointed by John Stott

A. All Souls pastoral staff 1950-1970

The following pastoral staff served under John Stott as Rector of All Souls. The list includes curates in All Souls and St Peter's, parish workers, leaders of the All Souls Clubhouse, student counsellors, and chaplains to the Oxford Street stores. From 1956 Frances assisted each of them in a range of ways.

For completeness, the list begins in 1950, when John Stott succeeded Harold Earnshaw-Smith as Rector. It concludes in 1970, when Michael Baughen assumed leadership of the church, and Frances handed over church admin responsibilities, to focus entirely on the work of the new Langham Trust.

From 1950 Gordon E Mayo (shortly to complete curacy); Sister Jordan (to 1957)

From 1951 F Donald B Eddison (to 1953); John T C B Collins (to 1957)

From 1953 Richard E H Bowdler (to 1958)

From 1954 C John E Lefroy (to 1965)

From 1956 G E F Rawlins (to 1965)

From 1957 Vera Williams (to 1965); Julian Charley (to 1964); Tom R Robinson (to 1962)

From 1958 Michael C Harper (to 1964)

From 1960 Martin G Peppiatt (to 1963)

From 1963 Peter Phenna (to 1969); O Miles Thomson (to 1967); Robert F H Howarth (to 1973 with a break for study)

From 1964 Peter B Bagnall (to 1967)

From 1965 George A R Swannell (to 1968); Michael J Wilcock (to 1969)

From 1966 Jo M Gardner (to 1971)

From 1967 Denis A Shepheard (to 1972)

From 1968 Ted A Schroder (to 1971)

From 1969 Barry Dawson (to 1973); Garry G Guinness (to 1972)

B. Study Assistants in 'the happy triumvirate'

Greg Scharf, Mark Hunt, Peggy Ward, Med Jackson and Ruth Adlam served as pastoral interns before the Study Assistant portfolio was formalized in 1977. Occasionally a short-term Study Assistant would stand in for a few months. These include Greg Downes (1993) and Jonathan Cranston (2002).*

Roy McCloughry 1977-78

Tom Cooper 1978-80

Mark Labberton 1980-81

Steve Ingraham 1981-1982

Bob Wismer 1982-1984

Steve Andrews 1984-1986

Toby Howarth 1986-1988

Todd Shy 1988-1992

Nelson Gonzalez 1993-1996

John Yates III ('JY') 1996-1999

Corey Widmer 1999-2002

Matthew Smith 2002-2005

Tyler Wigg Stevenson 2005-2006

Chris Jones ('CJ') 2006-2007

*Any others who served in this *locum* capacity are invited to contact the Publisher for their names to be added in a future printing.

APPENDIX 4
Press notices and Orders of service

PRESS NOTICES

Obituaries appeared in:

Langham Partnership News (7 June 2019)

The Times (10 June 2019)

Christian Today (11 June 2019)

Church Times (14 June 2019)

Church of England Newspaper (13 June 2019)

Fulcrum (25 June 2019)

Mid-Devon Advertiser, Bovey section (28 June 2019)

Ultimato magazine, Brazil (July 2019)

Evangelicals Now (August 2019)

Death notices were placed in *The Times, The Telegraph* (13 June 2019)

ORDERS OF SERVICE
[For the Thanksgiving and Committal services]

1. Thanksgiving service, 21 June 2019

All Souls, Langham Place, London (Service may be viewed on YouTube.)

Welcome: Revd Hugh Palmer, Rector

Opening hymn: Jesus! The Name high over all (Charles Wesley)

Reading: John 14: 1-21 Bishop Michael Nazir-Ali

Tributes:
Mark Labberton (on video), former John Stott Study Assistant
Heidi Cooper, Friend

Solo: Dear Child, I take you in my arms (The Song of Simeon)

Words: J R W Stott; Music: John Fear

Hymn: New every morning is the love (John Keble)

Tributes:
Julia Cameron, Friend and Biographer
Matthew Smith, Friend and former John Stott Study Assistant

Hymn: There is a hope that burns within my heart (Stuart Townend)

Prayers and the Lord's prayer: Revd Rico Tice, Friend

Readings:
Numbers 23:16-20 Mary Collins, Friend
Isaiah 55:6-11 Emily Bowerman, Friend, and John Stott's great niece

Solo: When I survey the wondrous cross (Isaac Watts)

Address: Revd Dr Chris Wright, International Ministries Director, Langham Partnership

Hymn: In Christ alone my hope is found (Townend / Getty)

Closing prayer and blessing: Revd Hugh Palmer

Organist and conductor: Dr Noel Tredinnick with the All Souls Instrumental Ensemble

Soloist: Elizabeth Robbings *Cellist for solo:* Mary Hall

2. Thanksgiving and Committal service, 1 July 2019

Church of St Peter, St Paul and St Thomas of Canterbury, Bovey Tracey

Welcome: Revd Graham Hamilton, Vicar

Introduction and sentences of scripture: Revd Dr Mark Labberton, President, Fuller Seminary and former John Stott Study Assistant

Hymn: Jesus! The Name high over all (Charles Wesley)

Reading: Matthew 25:14-24 Liz Wright, Friend

Tributes:
Eidi Cruz-Valdivieso, Friend
David Gallagher, Friend

Prayer and the Lord's Prayer: Roy McCloughry, Friend, and former John Stott Study Assistant

Reading: Philippians 2:1-11 Richard Padfield, cousin

Address: Revd Dr Mark Labberton

Hymn: In Christ alone my hope is found (Townend / Getty)

Closing prayer and blessing: Revd Dr Mark Labberton

Endnotes

Author's Preface

1 See Further Reading on p267.

2 *Oxford, By a Very Oxford Cat* (Dictum, 2019).

'The Archangel in charge of postings'

3 In a letter from Douglas Johnson, founding General Secretary of the Inter-Varsity Fellowship, now UCCF. For the full quote see Timothy Dudley-Smith *John Stott: The Making of a Leader* (p321).

4 *The Times, The Telegraph, The Independent* and *The Guardian* all carried obituaries on Friday, 29 July 2011.

Chapter 1

5 John Stott's funeral had taken place on 8 August 2011 in All Souls Church, Langham Place, London in a less-formal service for church family and for friends. His ashes were interred on 4 September 2011 in the churchyard in Dale, close to his writing retreat, The Hookses. (See Chapter 11.)

6 The commanding figure of Charles Simeon (1759-1836), Vicar of Holy Trinity Church, Cambridge, was famously captured in a series of silhouettes by Edouart Augustin. While divided by nearly 150 years, John Stott was, in a sense, tutored by Simeon in expository preaching.

7 The spelling 'virger' is used by St Paul's.

8 Tributes in the service were brought from senior leaders on all continents. The service may be found on YouTube.

[9] Timothy Dudley-Smith, retired Bishop of Thetford, was a friend from Cambridge days and John Stott's authorized biographer.

Chapter 2

[10] Claude Whitehead had a distinguished military career. He served with the 4th Kings Own Royal Lancaster Regiment (Rifles), and was awarded a DSO and the Chevalier Legion of Honour for bravery and leadership at the final battle in the Struma Valley, Salonica, in which he was wounded. He was twice mentioned in despatches and received the Military Cross for skilful leadership in extricating his men after the battle of Doiran. He played an active interest in local affairs, and was Assistant Area Officer (Newton Abbot division) of the Devon Special Constabulary. (Obituary, *The Paignton Observer*, 23 March 1944.)

[11] Annual dog show in the UK, dating back to 1886. Crufts awards are regarded as highly prestigious.

[12] The prayer for the day, as set out in the Book of Common Prayer (1662) which was widely used in all Anglican churches for another fifty years.

Chapter 3

[13] Pamela Hurle: *Malvern Girls' College: A Centenary History* p65 (Phillimore and Co Ltd, 1993).

[14] A term used in the UK to refer to some of the oldest-established schools offering an elite education.

Chapter 6

[15] Richard Westall RA (1765-1836). Based on the account of the trial in John's Gospel, and given to the Church by George IV.

[16] *Moses and the Brazen Serpent* by Augustus John (1978-1961). Permanent collection at University College, London (UCL) Arts Museum.

[17] See Numbers 21:9 and John 3:14-16.

18 Lorne Sanny (1920-2005) was to become the second President of the Navigators. Over his 30-year tenure in leadership, the work grew from a staff of 170 in fewer than a dozen countries to 2500 in 70 countries.

19 Many senior evangelical figures in Britain were converted through, or significantly shaped by, 'Bash camps', as they became known. The same work in Britain's leading schools continues today, now much expanded, under the name Titus Trust.

Interlude

20 Elizabeth Malleson, née Whitehead (1828-1916) wrote privately-published *Memoirs* providing rich and colourful vignettes. For Malleson's own achievements, in women's education and nursing, see the *Dictionary of National Biography.* Charles Mortimer Eastley traced his family back to 1600AD, based around the findings of the York Herald, the Hon Philip Carey, of the College of Arms, London. (Undated document, late 1960s. For family circulation only.)

21 The same day on which the battle is still remembered each year. An account by Colonel (later Major-General) Sir Alexander Dickson was presented to the Royal Regiment of Artillery, bearing out Maguire's extraordinary courage and leadership. A further account was published as *Memoirs of the Late War* by Captain John Cooke of the 43rd Regiment; and a painting presented to the Royal Academy by Prinsep Beadle in 1912. This he photographed, to send copies to the family.

22 Elizabeth Malleson *Memoirs*, 1926.

23 Ibid Introductory, p3.

24 After his death, Elizabeth, by then in her seventies, and living in Gloucestershire, compiled a selection of his letters home, to preserve his story. *In Memoriam Percy Whitehead* was privately printed in 1900.

25 The same regiment in which Francis Maguire and his son Francis had served.

[26] Established as three Fleurs de Lys, first used by Richard Eastleigh (1607-1665).

Chapter 7

[27] Frances Whitehead, while John Stott's personal secretary from the outset, covered a range of administrative tasks for the church. From 1970, when Michael Baughen first became Vicar of All Souls, her job title changed from All Souls Church Secretary to John Stott's Secretary.

[28] The Hookses would play a huge role in Frances's life. See Chapter 11.

[29] A friend of John Stott from Cambridge days. From 1980-1985 vicar of Holy Trinity, Brompton, home of the Alpha course; then a Prebendary of St Paul's Cathedral.

[30] A Harley Street cardiologist and Extra Physician to the Royal Household.

[31] See Ed Chris Wright *John Stott: A Portrait by his Friends* (IVP, 2011) p189.

[32] All Shirley's children and grandchildren are believers. One grandchild is named after Charles Simeon, which must have pleased Frances greatly. (See opening of Chapter 10.)

[33] Karen Blixen (1885-1962) is better known by her pen name, Isak Dinesen, for *Out of Africa* and *Babette's Feast*.

[34] Later married to Anna, and parents of Matthew Smith, introduced in Chapter 10.

[35] LAN for the local Langham exchange. All-figure dialling did not arrive until the mid 1960s.

[36] The sport of attempting to get past Frances would become a game for church staff. A curate under Michael Baughen recalled how curates would call Frances to ask for John, imitating the accents of Stott's senior international friends, who might just stand a chance of being allowed to interrupt him. The strike rate was low.

37 Cited in *The Times* obituary for Oliver Barclay.

38 See obituaries for DJ in *The Independent* on 11 Dec 1991 and *The Times* on 14 Dec 1991; and for Oliver Barclay in *The Times* on 4 Oct 2013 and *The Independent* on 25 Oct 2013.

39 Later to change its name to Church Leaders in Student Situations (CLISS), to incorporate the growing number of Polytechnics and Colleges of Education, which were later largely included in the university sector.

40 See Afterword: 'A Shared Legacy'.

41 Former missionary with the China Inland Mission (now OMF International) then Vice Principal of Oak Hill College.

Chapter 8

42 By 1970 the All Souls Clubhouse on Cleveland Street was well established, having been founded in 1958. It welcomed poorer families from the parish who would not feel comfortable in a church building. Today it would fall under the category 'Fresh expressions of Church'. John Stott was practising such fresh expressions decades before the phrase was coined.

43 This was a 'covenant with God and with each other'. The Congress was declared by *TIME* magazine (5 August 1974) as the most diverse gathering of Christians up to that time. The Covenant's 15 sections were to have deep and lasting influence, not least in the bringing together of evangelical confession and a commitment to social justice. John Stott's exposition and study guide to the Covenant was published the following year. It was agreed that the names of the Covenant's signatories would remain unpublished for 50 years. (Not everyone signed; some preferred an alternative covenant; some signed both.) A recording of Stott's presentation of the final text to the gathering may be found on *lausanne.org*.

44 It was for many years known by its original name, the Lausanne Committee for World Evangelization (LCWE).

[45] It was around the time that Frances began her job as Church Secretary that John Stott concluded that he should not marry, for the sake of his ministry. He had by that stage considered marriage on two occasions, but with both women had found himself unable to commit to that step. So after some careful heart searching, he had resolved that he would remain unmarried.

[46] Always referred to as JY. See Chapter 10.

[47] International Fellowship of Evangelical Students.

[48] David Pickard, OMF Thailand Director (and later OMF General Director), was part of the discussions on whether the conference should be relocated. Don Cormack had been one of the last missionaries to leave Phnom Penh when it fell to the Khmer Rouge in 1975, and one of the first to return. In the interim he and his wife, Margaret, ministered to those who managed to escape across the border into the camps.

[49] For a thoughtful and perceptive handling of the Cambodian story, see Don Cormack *Killing Fields, Living Fields: An unfinished portrait of the Cambodian Church: the church that would not die* (originally published by Monarch, 1997).

[50] For a detailed report and analysis of NEAC, see Timothy Dudley-Smith *John Stott: A Global Ministry,* pp275-278.

[51] Delivered on Monday, 2 May, 1988. Published with further refinements by the Church of England Evangelical Council (CEEC) as *NEAC3 'What is the Spirit saying...?' A Report from The National Evangelical Anglican Celebration* (1988).

Chapter 9

[52] Now Western University.

[53] See Lindsay Brown 'John Stott and the Student World' in Chris Wright et al *John Stott: Pastor, Leader and Friend* (Dictum, 2020).

[54] John Stott's sister, one year his senior, who died unexpectedly in 1979.

[55] Parents of Eidi. See Chapter 14.

[56] Daughter of René Padilla, whom John Stott had come to know well through IFES, and through his contribution to the Lausanne Congress in 1974.

Chapter 10

[57] The Cambridge Inter-Collegiate Christian Union. John Stott was deeply involved in this evangelical movement in his student days, and an honorary vice-president until he died.

[58] See Bill Lewis in Chris Wright et al *John Stott: Pastor, Leader and Friend* (Dictum edition, 2020).

[59] An aside to illustrate this: As was typical of all mealtimes at IFES conferences, speakers and leaders would eat with the students, and join them in standing in line for food. One particular mealtime demonstrated John Stott's humble spirit. At the 2003 IFES World Assembly in the Netherlands, Dutch students and young graduates acted as stewards for the event, arrayed in tee-shirts of their national orange. They had been assigned tasks to do, and they did them conscientiously. The steward checking ID at the dining hall that day was confronted with a problem. A white-haired gentleman, by this stage 82 years old, wanted to enter the hall without his Assembly name badge. Rules were rules. No-one could enter without ID. Uncle John, recognizing the Teutonic background and youthful inexperience of the rather over-zealous steward, stood aside. As various staff arriving for lunch guessed straight away what had happened, and offered advocacy, John shook his head with a grin and made a small waiving gesture with his hand. Matthew Smith, his Study Assistant, was in the meantime running to collect the missing lanyard.

[60] In 1986, now thirty years after Frances had 'crossed the road' from the BBC, she suffered a period of depression. She had flown over to Antrim in the early summer to see Rose, and to drive down with her to Galway, in the west of Ireland. Over the days Frances stayed with Rose and her sister in their Antrim home, Frances spent much time

in bed. It was not clear what had brought on this depression. When she flew back to England, she went to be with her mother in Bourne End, rather than returning to London. It was a worrying time for her friends and for her mother. This was the same year in which *The Cross of Christ* appeared, dedicated to Frances in honour of her thirty years of service. Given its subject matter, and the wide reach it would have, one wonders if, amid whatever insecurities may have been triggered in Frances, there might also have been an element of spiritual attack.

61 A permanent ferris wheel situated on the South Bank of The Thames, as part of the Millennium celebrations.

62 Her reflection on this in 2014 was typically self-deprecatory: 'This is nonsense. All I can do is type. Fast.'

63 CMS missionaries in Zaire. Wendy Toulmin was later invited to lead Langham Partnership in the South Pacific.

64 Former Chairman and long-serving board member of John Stott Ministries/USA, now known as Langham Partnership, USA.

65 Vivienne Curry, a former member of All Souls and at one stage an assistant to Frances Whitehead, previously served as a secretary to Ronald Inchley at IVP.

66 Revelation 2:13.

Chapter 11

67 The fascinating story of the discovery of The Hookses and its eventual purchase by John Stott is told in Timothy Dudley-Smith *John Stott: The Making of a Leader* Chapter 14.

68 In the same year the ownership was transferred by deed of gift to the Langham Trust.

69 Later *The Message of 2 Timothy* (Bible Speaks Today series).

70 Annual letter to friends, January 1993.

71 David Gallagher told the story of Frances's overseeing of all matters relating to The Hookses in his tribute to her at the interment of her ashes. See note 102.

72 Ed John Stott, *Making Christ Known: Historic Mission Documents from The Lausanne Movement 1974-1989* (Paternoster Press 1996).

73 Two small vignettes of the way John Stott's work, and Frances's typing, gained wide and often-unplanned currency.

(i) Some months in advance of the 1998 update of *Issues Facing Christians Today*, the chapter on same-sex partnerships was published as a free-standing booklet by HarperCollins (UK) and Revell (US). Richard Bewes invited Stott to preach an abbreviated version of the material at All Souls, and, sensing the controversy that the issue would cause at the decennial Lambeth Conference in July 1998, Richard sent a tape of the sermon to nearly 1,000 bishops and archbishops of the Anglican Communion. (New Year Newsletter, 1998).

(ii) Six years later we find a report that the Turkish translation of *The Cross of Christ* reached eighth place on the best-seller list of a well-known secular Turkish book club. (Newsletter New Year 2004).

Chapter 12

74 Referring to a time when some five percent of school leavers went to university, with a minority of women among that number.

Chapter 13

75 Shelagh Brown, then Dick Lucas's secretary, served for many years as personal assistant to Prof Sir Norman Anderson.

76 The same who died aged 21 in the Forlorn Hope.

77 Rose McIlrath served on the board of the Dogs Trust, which brought her to London frequently.

78 In his commitment to a simple lifestyle, John Stott at times had only one presentable pair of shoes, so a cobbler who could repair them on a Saturday was a necessity.

[79] G K Chesterton, received into the Catholic Church in 1922, was evidently loved and valued, and St Teresa's has several memorials to him. The church houses his personal library, including annotated first editions of all his works.

[80] His Honour Judge David Turner, High Court Judge in Chelmsford Circuit, and for many years the Church Warden at All Souls; Prof John Wyatt, Emeritus Professor of Ethics and Perinatology at University College, London.

Chapter 14

[81] This engraving, by an unknown artist, often appears together with Augustin Edouart's famous set of silhouettes of Charles Simeon in the pulpit. It is depicted as 'Returning' in J E M Cameron, ed: *Charles Simeon of Cambridge: Silhouettes and Skeletons* (Wipf and Stock, 2019; Dictum/EFAC, 2021).

[82] A memorial service was later held at St Barnabas, where Richard Bewes spoke, Phillip Herbert led the prayers and the Warden, Father Howard Such gave a heartfelt tribute about the way John Stott had become a part of a community. In some quarters, he had at first been viewed with suspicion, but many had revised their opinion of the evangelical wing of the Church of England through the gracious way he accepted them as they were. Seats were reserved for St Barnabas staff and residents at All Souls, and again at St Paul's Cathedral.

[83] From Chris Wright's email to Langham Partnership supporters, 5 September 2011.

[84] On a memorial plaque to Charles Simeon, placed by the Congregation on the south side of the chancel in Holy Trinity Church, Cambridge.

[85] Frances spoke to the current author, then in the late stages of editing a new anthology, with contributions from those who had worked with John Stott in a range of contexts. Frances sensed its perceptive observations would add a unique facet to this project, and with Eidi Cruz-Valdivieso's permission, it first appeared a few weeks later in Chris Wright et al, *John Stott: Pastor, Leader and Friend*. Alongside it

was placed the photograph of the 'Uncle with a grandfather's face'. This same photograph would from then on hang in Frances's study in Bourne End.

Chapter 15

86 Jill Freeman, whom Frances first got to know in the mid-late 1980s, while Jill was serving with LICC, recalled telephone calls from Frances around midnight, to see if Jill was still watching a major snooker final.

87 In her late eighties, shortly after retiring, Frances's energy had begun to wane. Not long afterwards, she was diagnosed with breast cancer, but her treatment kept this under control.

88 A companion newspaper to *The Independent*, short and pithy, first launched in 2010.

89 Frances had known Jonathan since he was born, and he had acted as a *locum* in the Happy Triumvirate. He would become the Hollywood vet.

90 Tragically Eidi's father Saúl had died very suddenly while Matthew and Eidi were on their honeymoon. His death brought deep shock.

91 Shirley came up to London from Ilkley for Frances's 60th birthday in 1985, and would call to see her in Weymouth Street whenever she was in London. On her final visit to Weymouth Street, Frances explained that John wasn't well and was resting, but she would see if he was able to come downstairs. He did come, and as he shook Shirley's hand it was, in Shirley's words, 'a final benediction on my visits to 12 Weymouth Street.'

92 Frances's third executor was Geoffrey Hill, who had been co-executor with Frances for John Stott's Will, having acted for both of them for many years.

93 There were naturally memories of John Stott's death in everyone's mind. Emily had been with her great uncle in the College of St Barnabas when he died eight years earlier, together with her mother, Caroline. Frances was also there, and Matthew Smith, and Eidi

Cruz-Valdivieso. Rose had received a call that morning from Frances before she left for St Barnabas; and the present author had received news late afternoon, to ensure all broadsheet obituaries were in place and broadsheet editors informed.

Chapter 16

[94] Available on YouTube.

[95] The Whitleys of Welstor Farm were related through the marriage of Claude Whitehead's sister, Elizabeth to William Whitley. Nigel Padfield's father had married one of William's younger sisters.

[96] See Frances Whitehead's full account in ed Chris Wright *John Stott: A portrait by his friends* (IVP, 2011).

[97] Numbers 23:16-20 and Isaiah 55:6-11.

[98] The Bovey Tracey Heritage Trust was set up in 1995, and the Heritage Centre, based in the town's old railway station, was opened in 2004.

[99] This photograph appeared on each of the orders of service for the All Souls Thanksgiving, and for the graveside committal.

[100] *Basic Christianity* was translated into over fifty languages. The ripples from it were and are far-reaching. These stories stand for countless others around the world.

[101] Christian influence in the Padfield line could be traced back to at least the 18th century. A fly-leaf in a book belonging to Joseph Padfield, dated 15 June 1862, described his parents, Benjamin and Susannah Padfield, as 'staunch Methodists their whole lives', and states that '[John] Wesley was entertained on many occasions' in his grandfather's home, also Joseph Padfield, in Holcombe, Somerset.

[102] This tribute, bringing a unique aspect on Frances's responsibility for The Hookses, is available in full on *dictumpress.com*.

[103] Matthew 25:14-24 and Philippians 2:1-11.

Afterword

[104] David Jones (father of CJ, John Stott's last Study Assistant) was then President of what is now Langham Partnership US. It was previously known as John Stott Ministries.

[105] Its launch lecture by John Stott earlier in the year drew 70% of the nation's parliamentarians.

[106] See *The Times* 'Lives Remembered', 8 August 2011, the same day as John Stott's funeral.

[107] The Literary Executors own copyright for seventy years after an author's death and give permission for reproduction. John Stott's book royalties were assigned to Langham Partnership, and when books are published commercially the Executors ensure that this ministry receives appropriate benefit. The Executors work with publishers to achieve the widest possible distribution of content in many languages. They also arrange new editions, something which Stott himself encouraged.

Giving permission for other-language publishing is a big responsibility, for the publisher must demonstrate good judgment in his translators, who need to grasp both the substance and the nuance of the text.

[108] Prof John Wyatt took the chair from 2014.

[109] See 'An Abrahamic and Apostolic Ministry', in Chris Wright et al *John Stott: Pastor, Leader and Friend*' (2012; Dictum expanded edition, 2020)

[110] See obituaries for Ronald Inchley in *The Independent* 14 May, 2005; *The Times* 25 May 2005. John Stott was to publish most of his books with IVP, a publishing house founded by the Inter-Varsity Fellowship (now UCCF) which would nurture evangelical publishing in many nations, through sister movements in IFES. It was student ministry with IFES that had first drawn Stott overseas. Now these student movements were to prove a major channel for his writing.

111 The Rt Revd John Hayden, later Assistant Bishop of Mount Kilimanjaro, worked on an honorary basis for ELT from 1983-1996. With the barest of administrative costs and Hayden's driven passion, the ELT annual income of £25,000 would, by the mid-1990s, grow to £500,000. John Hayden oversaw the production of the first book catalogues in English, French, Spanish and Portuguese.

112 Langham Literature is working with others to nurture a new generation of evangelical writers and editors, and to encourage the growth of publishing houses in over twenty nations.

113 From 2013 this became a joint role with the directorship of the International Council for Evangelical Theological Education (ICETE), continuing to work closely with their sister organization, Overseas Council.

114 Jonathan Lamb served with UCCF and then as IFES Regional Secretary for Europe and Eurasia, and IFES Associate General Secretary before joining the staff of Langham Partnership.

115 Part One comprises a Confession of Faith, crafted in the language of covenantal love, and Part Two, a Call to Action. Chris Wright had shared his thinking with John Stott about the way it should be fashioned, and wrote much of it at John's desk at The Hookses.

116 The Universities and Colleges Christian Fellowship, formerly the Inter-Varsity Fellowship (IVF). The shared office at 5 Blue Boar Street, Oxford, adjoining the Town Hall, and in the heart of the university, was opened in July 2012.

117 For example 'DJ's' (after Douglas Johnson), 'the Doctor's' (after Martyn Lloyd-Jones), the Barclay Room and 'The Press' (after Inter-Varsity Press).

118 See contributions by several in Chris Wright et al: *John Stott: Pastor, Leader and Friend:* (Dictum edition, 2020).

119 A major introductory article was published in *The Churchman* in the first quarter of 1962.

[120] For a full account of this, see Chapter 7 of Timothy Dudley-Smith: *John Stott: The Making of a Leader* (also more briefly told in Chapter 3 of Roger Steer: *Inside Story*).

[121] Vincezi Imondi, a carpenter from Switzerland, had met Mercy while he was serving on a team of short-term volunteers in India.

[122] For further news of the Mahalir Aran Trust and the Eastgate Church, go to *mahalirarantrust.com*

Appendix 2(ii)

[123] IVP UK and IVP US *John Stott: The Making of a Leader* (1999) and *John Stott: A Global Ministry* (2001)

Further Reading

John Stott: The Making of a Leader (IVP, 1999) and *John Stott: A Global Ministry* (IVP, 2001) by Timothy Dudley-Smith. Authorized biography in two volumes. Masterly. Very readable, and comprehensively annotated and indexed.

John Stott: A Portrait by his Friends ed: Chris Wright (IVP, 2011). Published for John Stott's 90th birthday.

John Stott: Pastor, Leader and Friend by Chris Wright, Lindsay Brown, Samuel Escobar, et al (Dictum/EFAC, 2020)

Charles Simeon of Cambridge: Silhouettes and Skeletons ed J E M Cameron. (Wipf and Stock, USA, 2019; Dictum/EFAC, 2021) Traces Simeon's influence to the present day.

For children:

John Stott: Call me 'Uncle John' by Julia Cameron (Dictum / EFAC, 2021). Fun, authorized biography for children with timeline, maps and 25 Fascinating Facts.

Dictum titles include:

Oxford and Cambridge Reformation Walking Tour by Julia Cameron (Dictum/Day One, 2019)

The Leadership Files: From around the world, across a century by Vaughan Roberts, Ajith Fernando et al. with Appendix on Good Governance. (Dictum/EFAC, 2020)

The Cross: A fresh look at the meaning of the death of Christ by James Philip (Dictum/EFAC, 2019)

Money and the Gospel: Giving money with grace; Handling money with integrity by John Stott and Chris Wright (Dictum/EFAC, 2019)

Authority and Joy: The Bible in your life by John Stott and Sinclair Ferguson. Includes the widely-used McCheyne Bible Reading Plan (Dictum/EFAC, 2021)

Oxford, By a Very Oxford Cat by Julia Cameron, in a rather different vein. About a cat whom Frances Whitehead named Simeon (Dictum, 2019)

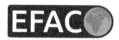

EFAC Global was founded in 1961 by John Stott as the Evangelical Fellowship in the Anglican Communion. Its role has become even more critical in recent years.

Through local fellowships, EFAC serves to encourage and develop biblical literacy, vital to healthy doctrine and practice, and effective mission, to build '*Bible People. Gospel People. Church People.*' EFAC works to equip leaders to stand firm, to engage thoughtfully with secular trends, and to articulate a persuasive biblical response. Its affiliated group in England is the Church of England Evangelical Council.

EFAC's Theology Resource Network (TRN) draws senior theologians from all continents. As John Stott was always keen to remind EFAC's early members, Christ gave gifts to his church to share. Through the TRN's international membership, insights from many contexts are shared around the table, and then shared more widely through gatherings and in print.

Christ prayed in Gethsemane for the future church to be unified; 'at one' with its Apostolic roots (John 17:20ff). EFAC, under the leadership of an International Council and General Secretary, and through its Theology Resource Network, local fellowships and small team, seeks to further true unity.

To learn more, visit *efacglobal.com*